LAND AND LABOUR IN A DECCAN VILLAGE

LAND AND LABOUR IN A DECCAN VILLAGE

HAROLD H. MANN

GYAN

Published by

GYAN

Gyan Publishing House
5, Ansari Road
Daryaganj, New Delhi-110002
Phone: 011-47034999, 9811692060
E-mail: books@gyanbooks.com

Distribution Network
gyanbooks.com
India, USA, Canada, UK, Australia

ISBN: 978-93-7447-219-4 (PB)

First Published, 1917

2nd Impression 2026

Printed at: Gyan Press, Delhi.

LAND AND LABOUR IN A DECCAN VILLAGE
Author: HAROLD H. MANN

LAND AND LABOUR IN A DECCAN VILLAGE.

BY

HAROLD H. MANN, D.Sc.,
Principal, Poona Agricultural College,

IN COLLABORATION WITH

D. L. SAHASRABUDDHE, B.Sc., L.Ag.,
N. V. KANITKAR, B.Sc., B.Ag.,
V. A. TAMHANE, B.Sc., L.Ag.,
AND OTHERS.

HUMPHREY MILFORD,
OXFORD UNIVERSITY PRESS,
LONDON AND BOMBAY.

1917.

PREFACE.

During the last few years there has been constantly increasing interest in the economic problems of rural India. That these are special in character, and not by any means analogous to those of many other countries is very obvious to those who have made even a superficial study of the question.

As regards the Deccan, interest in the matter was quickened some years ago by the appearance of Keatinge's "Rural Economy in the Bombay Deccan," a book which for the first time collected together and reviewed the available data with regard to the economic history and present economic position of the rural population of the western portion of the large central plateau of peninsular India. This book was in the highest sense stimulating. One felt, in reading it, that the author had raised a large number of questions which urgently demanded solution, and had pointed out the method of local close detailed study which alone could give the solution demanded. One felt, on the other hand, that many of the conclusions at which Keatinge arrived were extremely doubtful, not because of the fault of his methods, but on account of the inadequacy of his data.

It seemed, in fact, that the close study of a single village might give helpful data in approaching many of the matters which arise when any of the numerous economic and economic-agricultural questions in the Deccan are considered. And on suggesting to my assistants at the Poona Agricultural College that such a close study of a single village would be valuable, they volunteered to carry it out. Led by Messrs. D. L. Sahasrabuddhe, B.Sc., L.Ag., N. V. Kanitkar, B.Sc., B.Ag., V. A. Tamhane, B.Sc., L.Ag., they undertook the very long, laborious, and painstaking investigation of which an account is given in the following pages.

The village which came under investigation was chosen (1) as being near enough to Poona to be accessible, and yet as being largely out of the immediate influence of a large town; (2) as being typical of a large tract in the districts of the Deccan where the *kharif* or rains crop is the most important, and where, hence, the rains are more certain than they are further east; (3) as being one where the influence of irrigation, whether from canals or wells was all but negligible.

The various parts of the inquiry were specially made by the following gentlemen, and to them I tender my very sincere thanks for the care which they have given to the obtaining of the data:—

Mr. D. L. Sahasrabuddhe—Geology, Sociology, Holdings, Cattle, and the following crops, Carrots, Peas, Sugarcane.

Mr. N. V. Kanitkar—Drainage, Sociology, Holdings and the following crops, Jowar, Sugarcane.

Mr. V. A. Tamhane—Soils, Holdings, and, among crops, Wheat.

Mr. D. M. Ranade—Manures, Implements, and, among crops, Bajri and its mixtures.

Mr. V. G Patwardhan—Drainage, Soils, and, among crops, Groundnut.

Mr. D. D. Abhyankar—Waters, and, among crops, Gram.

Mr. S. R. Paranjpe—Rotations and mixtures of crops.

Mr. S. R. Deshmukh—Manures, Implements.

Mr. R. K. Bhide—Weeds.

The late Mr. G. D. Mehta.—Seeds,

HAROLD H. MANN.

TABLE OF CONTENTS.

PLATE I.
(*Frontispiece.*)

A general view of the village of Pimpla Soudagar from the river side.

CHAPTER I.

INTRODUCTION.

THE Bombay Deccan is almost entirely a rural tract, but it may be divided in this sense into two sections of very different agricultural character. Though the line of division is not very definite, it runs roughly north and south a few miles to the east of Poona, and hence about fifty to sixty miles east of the ridge of the Western Ghats. East of this line the country forms a tract of extremely uncertain rainfall, where the rainfall in June, July and the early part of August is not very heavy, and where the rain, largely from local storms, which comes in September and early October is that on which the cultivators most largely depend for growing their crops. It is essentially therefore a *rabi* tract, that is to say, one which depends chiefly on the crops sown in September and October and reaped in January, February and March. In this area the rainfall never exceeds thirty inches and is more commonly twenty-five inches or below, and very uncertain.

In this *rabi* tract the spurs of the Western Ghats rapidly become less prominent on proceeding to the east. The country while still hilly and the land undulating is far more cultivable as a whole than the district further to the west. The area of rocky soil becomes less, the soil becomes deeper and stiffer, and but for the uncertainty of the rainfall, the country would be one of the finest agricultural tracts of peninsular India.

The country to the west of the imaginary line is of a very different character. Here the rainfall is far more certain, and as one proceeds towards the west it becomes very much heavier, until on the ridge of the Western Ghats we reach places where the rainfall is heavier than almost anywhere in the world. Near Poona, however, the rain is still moderate in amount:

at that city the average amounts to about thirty inches per annum. The heaviest rainfall, however, occurs in June and July, that in September being distinctly less, and over almost the whole of this tract the staple crops are those raised during the rainy season itself.

This is due to the fact that the September rain is small, and perhaps, also, even more, to the fact that the soils are on the average shallower and less retentive than further to the east.

In this tract of *kharif* or rains crops the country is rugged, bare, and very hilly. The uplands are almost bare of soil, and the villages and the cultivation usually occur in valleys where the soil has been washed and has been deposited in pockets which fill the hollows. We have in fact an alternation of barren country, hardly even capable of growing herbage for pasture, with rock almost at the surface,—and smiling valleys with deep soil, generally with wells, and a general appearance of prosperity. The rivers are largely rocky torrents, running to the east, and these often (except in the bigger cases) are almost dry for a great part of the year except in long pools. The village cultivation often owes its existence to some ridge of rock which has prevented the soil from the higher lands being washed into the river, and still protects it from the incursion of the river torrents during the rainy season.

The rainfall in this tract is perhaps well exemplified by that of Poona lying almost at its eastern limit, and Vadgaon lying near its centre, where the rainfall is becoming very heavy and where rice is grown. The village we are to consider lies between these, but approximates much more closely to the Poona conditions than to the other. Its actual distance from Poona is eight, that from Vadgaon is sixteen, miles :—

RAINFALL OF POONA.

	1906 Ins.	1907 Ins.	1908 Ins.	1909 Ins.	1910 Ins.	1911 Ins.	1912 Ins.	1913 Ins.	1914 Ins.	1915 Ins.	Average 10 years. Ins.
January ..	0.02	0.02	..	0.02	..	..	..	..	..	..	..
February	..	..	..	..	..	..	..	..	..	..	..
March ..	..	0.10	..	..	..	..	..	..	..	0.02	0.01
April ..	..	2.85	0.43	..	..	..	..	0.87	..	1.65	0.58
May ..	..	..	..	1.48	0.19	..	0.51	1.59	..	..	0.48
June ..	8.04	5.13	2.23	4.65	6.88	5.96	1.85	14.63	7.19	14.01	7.06
July ..	3.33	16.52	6.35	5.86	2.18	1.26	10.62	3.85	13.54	10.27	7.38
August ..	4.12	7.05	4.85	1.46	9.51	7.04	2.01	2.01	6.36	2.03	4.64
September.	1.99	9.21	8.01	3.30	5.66	0.14	0.45	2.53	4.93	6.48	4.27
October ..	0.60	0.57	0.70	1.63	5.22	0.25	8.41	1.37	0.83	1.41	2.10
November..	0.40	0.04	0.75	..	2.83	2.50	2.84	..	0.86	0.94	1.12
December..	0.02	..	..	..	..	0.19	..	..	0.02	..	0.02
Total..	18.52	41.49	23.32	18.30	32.47	17.34	26.69	26.85	33.73	36.81	27.66

RAINFALL OF VADGAON.

	1906 Ins.	1907 Ins.	1908 Ins.	1909 Ins.	1910 Ins.	1911 Ins.	1912 Ins.	1913 Ins.	1914 Ins.	1915 Ins.	Average 10 years. Ins.
January ..	..	..	..	..	..	..	..	..	..	..	..
February	..	..	..	..	..	..	..	..	..	..	..
March ..	..	0.54	..	..	..	..	..	..	..	..	0.05
April ..	..	3.23	..	..	..	..	..	0.83	..	1.71	0.59
May ..	..	..	..	0.78	..	..	..	1.82	..	..	0.26
June ..	8.55	6.24	2.22	5.57	10.46	7.30	2.05	26.51	7.16	13.73	8.98
July ..	11.01	21.57	17.08	17.96	9.05	2.97	22.27	11.62	30.49	19.50	16.35
August ..	8.64	19.46	7.61	2.70	15.29	12.76	8.48	6.68	14.99	7.62	10.42
September	4.66	4.14	9.07	4.34	3.18	1.76	2.04	5.57	8.94	12.94	5.66
October ..	0.79	0.77	0.88	2.13	6.15	0.80	4.66	2.24	1.06	0.50	2.00
November..	0.07	..	0.17	..	1.06	2.15	1.63	..	0.76	0.72	0.66
December..	..	..	..	..	..	..	..	..	..	..	..
Total..	33.72	55.95	37.03	33.48	45.19	27.74	41.13	55.27	63.40	56.72	44.97

PLATE II.
(To face Page 5.)

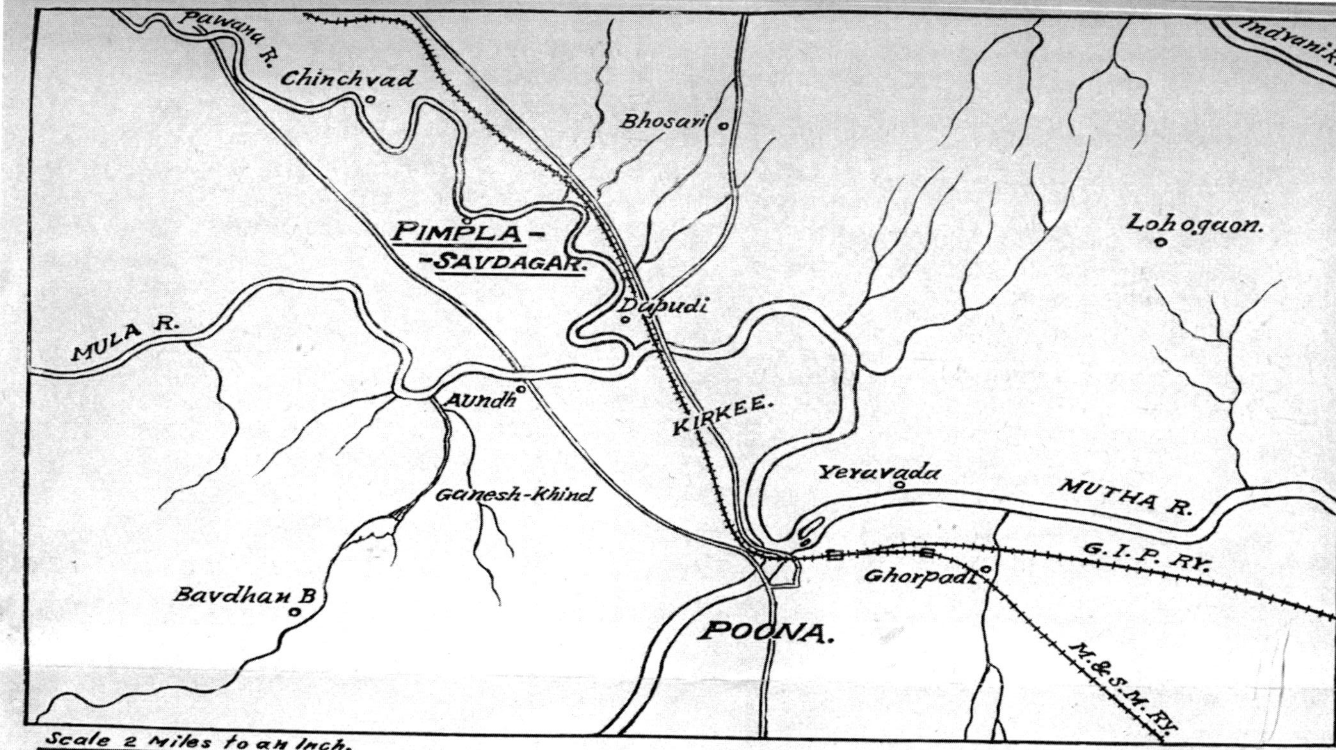

Position of the Village of Pimpla Soudagar in relation to Poona.

The village of Pimpla Soudagar, with which the present study is concerned, lies in the second of these tracts, that is to say, its rainfall is chiefly in June and July, and a considerable proportion of its crops are grown during the rainy season itself. It is placed on the banks of the Pawana river, which joins the Moola at Kirkee, and is about eight miles north-west of Poona. It has thus, probably, a rainfall slightly heavier than that of Poona, but of the same general character. It lies at an elevation of about 1,820 feet above the sea.

Poona is its market, and Kirkee to a smaller extent. Some of its people go to Poona for work, and a larger number to the factories at Kirkee, distant five miles. It lies almost midway between the present Poona-Bombay road, *via* Kirkee, and the old Poona-Bombay road, *via* Aundh, and both of these are used for the carriage of produce.

The area of the village land (what would be called the parish in an English countryside) is 1,065 acres. All is held under the ordinary *ryotwari* tenture of the Deccan, but the *inam* rights (or ownership of the land with a right to the whole or a portion of the land assessment) of 214 acres are held by private inamdars, while there is a charge against the revenue of the whole village dating from 1819 A.D. There are few wells and hardly any irrigation, and, in fact, it is a typical village with practically no irrigation of the part of the Deccan in which it lies.

In order to get a full picture of village life in the Western Deccan it must be remembered that two other types of village would have to be considered. These are (1) the kind of village which possesses a large number of wells for irrigation, and in which the prosperity or otherwise of the village depends on the existence of these wells, and (2) the kind of village which is a creation of irrigation canals, in which cultivation is rich with an intensity such as is rarely to be seen in any other large area in India.

The primary object of the present study is, however, to try and present a picture of the economic position of a village chiefly, if not entirely, dependent on the rainfall, in the Western Deccan, and we must leave for future study the other types which we have specified. In connection with Pimpla Soudagar we will therefore consider in order—

I. The physical character, geology, and topography, soils, subsoils, water, and drainage of the village.

II. The division of the land, and the holdings.

III. The vegetation, crops and cultivation of the village.

IV. The agricultural stock.

V. The population of the village and the character and occupation of the people.

VI. The general conclusions to be drawn from our study.

CHAPTER II.

The Physical Characters of the Village of Pimpla Soudagar.

A.—Geological Characters.

Almost the whole of the Bombay Deccan consists of a plateau whose average elevation is a little under 2,000 feet, sloping very gently to the east, which owes its origin to one of the largest and longest series of volcanic phenomena that has occurred in geological history. The rocks are hence entirely volcanic in character, and consist of what is usually termed 'Deccan Trap.' 'Deccan Trap' is not, however, a term which implies anything very definite in point of composition or structure. It results from a long series of eruptions, the lava from each of which is spread out over that which had occurred previously. Each lava flow was many feet thick, and on cooling formed rock of very different character in the various parts of the layer. In the lower part, where it cooled slowly and under great pressure, the rocks formed were very hard, highly crystalline, with an exceedingly dense structure; in the upper part of each flow, on the other hand, where the cooling was more rapid and the pressure was less, the rocks produced were much softer, contained very frequent cavities and fissures, and were hence much more subject to decay and hence to denudation as a result of the action of air and water, or both combined. More than this, in the interval between the lava flows, the upper part of the preceding layer of lava became oxidised, and hence soft, was washed down by rain into such hollows as existed, and became the home of plants and possibly even of forests before being covered up and the vegetation destroyed by another layer of lava, which ultimately became another layer of trap rock.

This geological origin accounts very largely for the topography of the Deccan. Rapid decay of the surface layers of the successive beds of lava, and hence the formation of material which could easily be washed away and carried to fill up other hollows at lower levels; permanence of the hard rocks forming the lower layers with very slow denudation where a surface of such character is exposed. We have thus, as already described, a country of the most contradictory character. Whenever a hollow existed, it has been filled with the washings from the decay of the higher lands, giving a rich valley; the higher lands themselves have been washed bare until a hard layer of rock has been reached, and this has remained with extremely slow further denudation.

This condition of things is perhaps characteristic, in general lines, of all rocky regions. But in the Deccan the transition from the bare rocky uplands to the smiling valleys with deep soil is sharper than almost anywhere. A few yards will separate sometimes a piece of bare rock giving at the most a very thin grass herbage, and a rich deep black soil capable of growing the biggest and finest crops of sugarcane. We have passed along a road where there was rock on one side, and a crop of sugarcane giving a yield of thirty to forty tons per acre on the other. And such cases abound.

The villages are nearly always in a hollow into which the washings from the uplands have gathered, and this is the case with the village of Pimpla Soudagar, which we have studied. This is situated (see map) on the banks of the river Pawana, a tributary of the Moola which passes Kirkee and Poona and ultimately falls into the Bhima. Its water reaches the east coast by the Krishna. The boundaries of the village land on three sides—east, south, and south-west—are situated at a slightly higher level with bare exposures of rock and the so-called '*mal*' land which constitutes the first product of the decay of the rocks still too coarse in texture to have been

PLATE III.
(*To face Page* 9.)

Place where the Pawana **river** has cut through the rock on leaving the village area.

carried completely into the lower levels. Further, there is a ridge of rock of lower level which crosses the river at the point at which it leaves the village, and whose existence has made possible the deposit of the soil in the village area.

The river itself is little else than a rocky torrent, which reaches the village from the north-west. Through the greater part of the village land its bed is about one hundred feet broad. During the dry season this remains filled with water owing to the interposition of the rocky ridge already referred to, to the east of the village site. At this point the river becomes narrower, and cuts its way through the rock in three narrow streams, which become powerful rapids in the rainy season when the river completely covers the rocks. The strength of the current at this point can, at other times of the year, be judged by the large number of potholes which are found there. In a length of two hundred and forty feet, the river being forty feet wide, there are eighty-seven potholes varying in size from small cavities to large tublike hollows. Some of the larger are over five feet deep with a diameter of four feet. Some of these have smaller subsidiary potholes in them, and the wearing has been so great that some of these have cut away the rock inside and established communication with the outside river.

These facts indicate the powerful nature of the torrent which the river forms in the rains. The ridge of rock, however, has allowed the deposit of much stone and gravel on the flatter stretch of water which lies opposite the greater part of the village. This contains large quantities of water-worn stones consisting of amygdaloidal trap, rock crystal, chalcedony, agate, moss-agate, carnelian, bloodstone, flints, opal, jasper, banded jasper, felspar, zeolites, many of them covered with layers of green glauconite.

The village exists as a cultivated area partly, as we have remarked, on account of the ridge of rock near the point where the river leaves it, and partly because along the greater part of the bank of the river a rocky ridge exists parallel to the bank, which has prevented the washing away of the soil and silt which has been deposited behind it. This is, of course, pierced where the *nalas* enter the river, but along most of the river bank it exists though usually under a layer of soil, and it is on this that the houses and the *gaothan* (or village site) are placed. The existence of this is illustrated well by the sections of the land taken (see Plate 3) which show it at a very small depth near the river bank in the east and centre of the village. The existence of such a ridge of rock near to and parallel with the river probably occurs in many places in the Deccan and accounts for the planting of so many villages on high land near a river, while lower land occurs further from the river bed and would hardly form a suitable village site.

We have thus village land lying as it were in a basin. Round the area is higher rocky land on the west, south, and south-east. There is a well-marked ridge of rock near the banks of the river and parallel to it, higher than the land behind it.

The basin is, however, [as is well shown in section No. 4 (line G. H., Plate 3) which goes from west to east] not a regular one, and a ridge with the rock much nearer the surface of the soil crosses the middle of the village from north to south, and gives an area with much shallower soil than the rest. The deep soil of the western part of the village continues into the next village which lies to the west. The whole area, in fact, consists of a double hollow filled with silt partly from the river and partly by direct washing from the higher land round about. The depth of the resulting soil and the coarseness or fineness of its character depends on the depth of the original hollow in the rock, and the extent to which the water was calm during deposit. As the rocky barrier to the course of the river torrent has been cut away, the basinlike character has become less obvious, but it still can be seen in a study of the sections shown. In the western part of the area denudation now exceeds deposition and the alluvial material formerly deposited now tends to be cut up and carried way (as we shall

Plate IV.
(To face Page 11.)

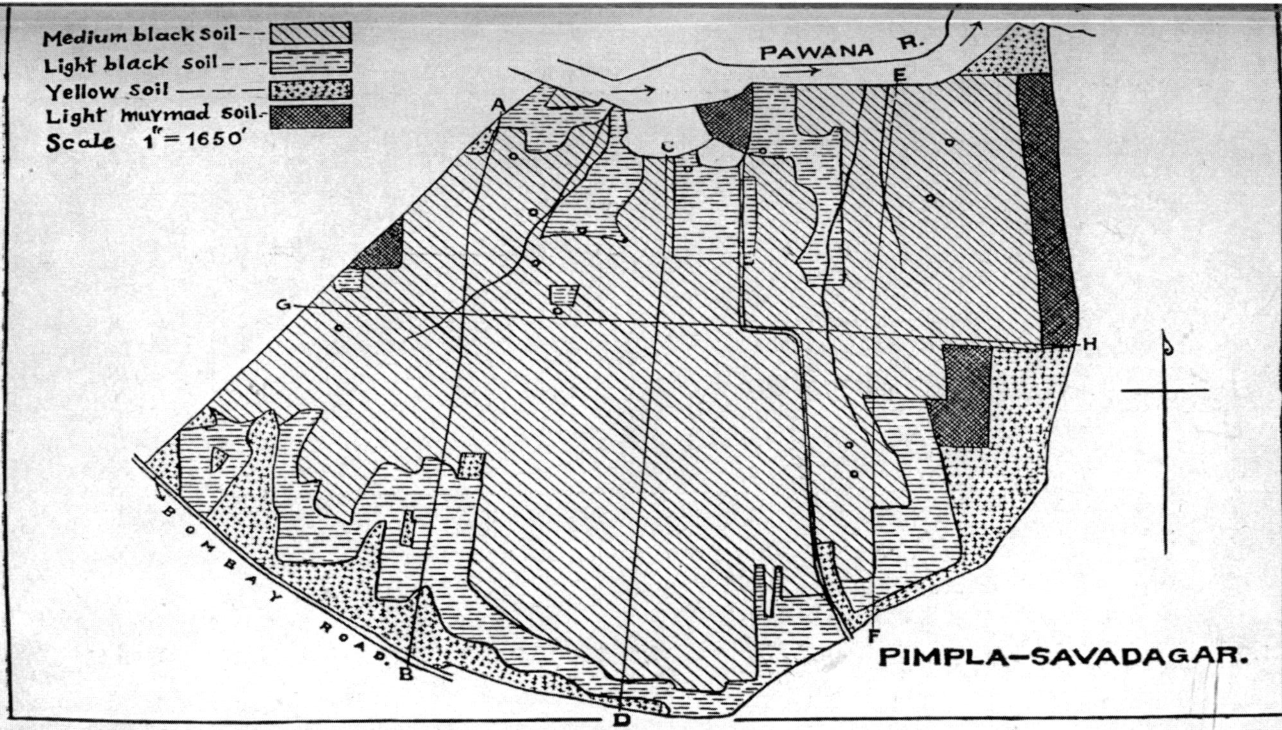

Soil Map of the Village of Pimpla Soudagar.

(*Sections on lines AB., CD., EF., & GH., are shown in Plates V & VI.*)

see later). But the origin of the village is still obvious and reflects itself in the character of the soils which we will now study.

B.—Soils of the Village.

From the above description of the rocks in the village and their arrangement, it will be easily understood that the soil and subsoil of a village like Pimpla Soudagar can be essentially divided into two materials. On the one hand there is the so-called *murum* which represents the material produced by the decay of the rock *in situ*, and which forms the subsoil almost throughout the village and occasionally appears at the surface, and the vast bulk of the surface soil whether yellow, brown, or black, which covers it and has in almost every case been carried to the spot by flowing water.

The *murum* layer, so commonly though not universally found between the rock and the actual surface soil in the Deccan, is particularly abundant and universal in this village. This would be expected, as the actual rock exposures show that the rock in the village is near the surface of a lava flow and is hence of a highly amygdaloidal and quickly weathering type. This is also shown by the fact that some, at any rate, of the rock is porphyritic, the large glassy felspar crystals being very well developed.

As is well known, this *murum* layer which underlies the soil itself and which, as already stated, is formed by the decay of the trap rock *in situ*, is a porous material, containing much half-decayed rock which is usually penetrable by plant roots but is usually too dry to be of much use as a subsoil in the arid conditions of the Deccan. This is so much the case that the value of the soil is usually considered as depending on its depth to the *murum* layer, the latter itself being ignored.

In the village of Pimpla Soudagar this *murum* is exposed and forms the soil in a limited area on the higher land at the east of the village (*murmad*), and on another area on the south-west where it is shallower and forms what has been classed as yellow soil. These two varieties of soil may be described as follows :—

Murmad soil.—This variety of soil is found on the eastern boundary of the area, adjoining the village of Pimpla-gurav. A portion that borders the rocky banks of the Pawana river is also of this type. It is a poor dry soil, from four to six inches deep, overlying a subsoil of hard *murum* into which plant roots hardly penetrate. Its colour varies from yellow to blackish. As will be easily seen, such a soil practically consists of the upper layer of the *murum*, which is worked, and it forms a hungry dry soil. But with careful tillage it gives, in a favourable season and during the rains, a fair produce of such crops as *bajri* (*Pennisetum typhoideum*), *tur* (*Cajanus indicus*), and *niger* (*Guizotia abyssinica*). A good part of the area is, however, considered as not worth cultivating and is used as a grazing ground, though the grass is very thin.

A typical specimen of such soil gave on a physical analysis the following results :—

Coarse sand and Gravel.	(Over .16 mm in diameter).	17.48%
Fine Sand	..(.07 mm to .16 mm ,,)	60.78%
Coarse Silt.	..(.03 mm to .07 mm ,,)	11.35%
Medium Silt	..(.01 mm to .03 mm ,,)	4.21%
Fine Silt	..(.008 mm to .01 mm ,,)	3.07%
Finest Silt and Clay.	less than .008 mm ,,)	3.11%

These figures are enough to show the very dry character of the soil, and hence its adaptability only to plants which grow actually during the rainy season, and to them only when the rain is regular and well timed.

A partial chemical analysis of a typical sample of this soil gave figures as follows :—

Sand and insoluble Silicates	79.96%
Loss on Ignition	8.06%

PLATE V.
(To face Page 12.)

SECTIONS SHOWING THE SOIL & SUBSOIL LEVELS AT PIMPLA-SAUDAGAR.

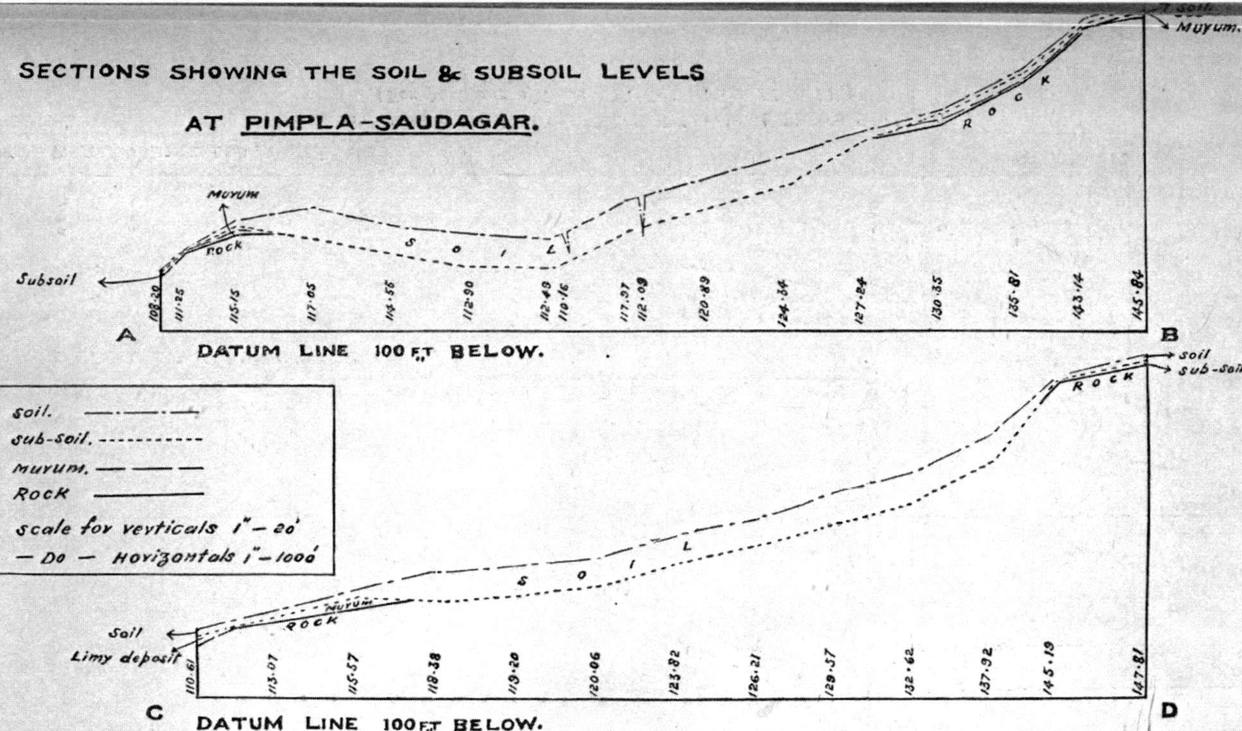

(For positions o lines AB. & CD. see Plate IV.)

PLATE VI.
(To face Page 13.)

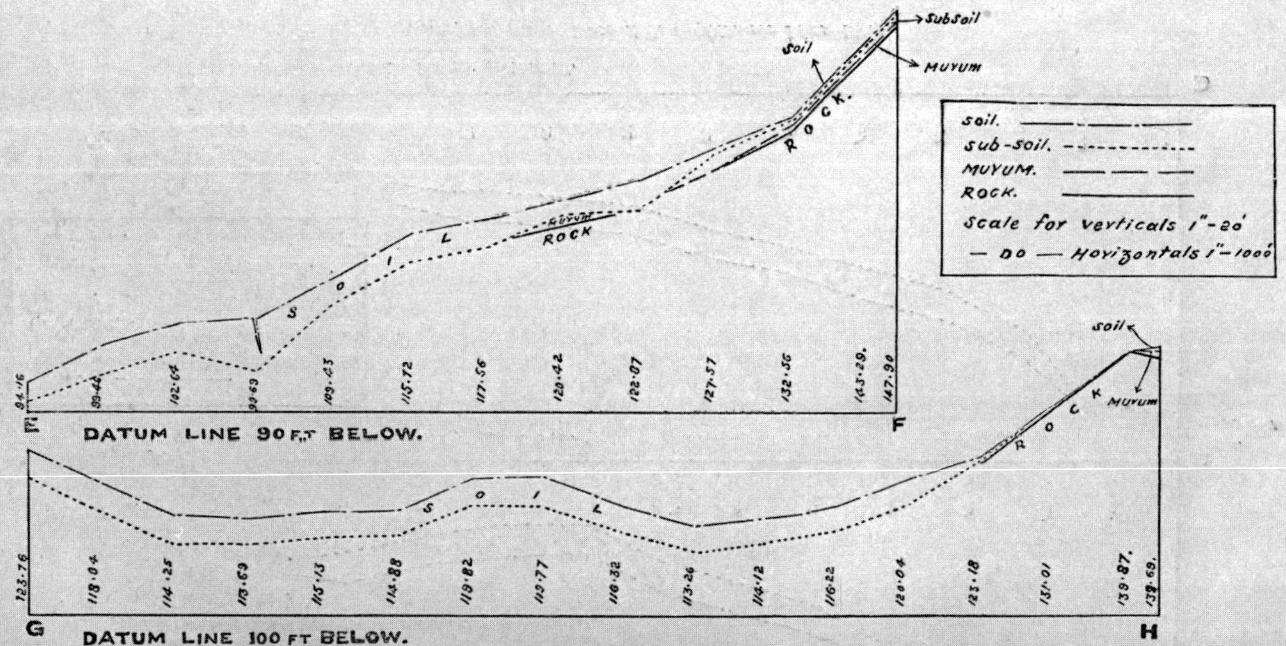

Sections showing the Soil and Sub-Soil Levels at Pimpla Soudagar.
(*For positions of lines EF. & GH. see Plate IV.*)

Organic matter (by direct determination) *	..		..	0.82%
Nitrogen	..	..	..	0.05%
Phosphoric acid (P_2O_5)	..	..	..	0.11%
Potash (K_2O)	..	..	..	0.93%
Lime (Ca O)	..	..	..	0.80%

This soil is very poor in humus and hence in nitrogen; in other respects it is well furnished with plant food. Its excessive dryness seems, however, to prevent the development of organic matter, and so it remains, as do nearly all similar soils in the Deccan, a half-barren soil of low retentiveness and hence of extreme poverty.

Yellow soil :—This soil differs little from the *murmad* soil, except that lying on rock instead of on *murum* it is a still drier and more poverty-stricken material. It is found in large amount on the south-east boundary of the village. Its depth does not usually exceed four inches, and it lies over rock or a very rocky substratum. If cultivated at all, it is usually planted with *argadi jowar* (*Sorghum*) as a rains crop, but the greater portion is uncultivable and gives the poorest and barest of herbage.

The physical analysis of a typical specimen, as follows, shows the excessively hungry, dry nature of the land :—

Coarse sand and Gravel	..	(Over .16 mm in diameter)	.. 30.32%
Find Sand	..	(.07 mm to .16 mm ,,)	.. 50.99%
Coarse Silt	..	(.03 mm to .07 mm ,,)	.. 8.11%
Medium Silt	..	(.01 mm to .03 mm ,,)	.. 3.42%
Fine Silt	..	(.008 mm to .01 mm ,,)	.. 4.65%
Finest Silt and Clay	..	(Less than .008 mm. ,,)	.. 2.51%

The following figures show the results of a partial chemical analysis of a dried sample :—

* The organic carbon is directly determined and multiplied by 2·16.

Sand and insoluble Silicates	80.80%
Loss on ignition	7.40%
Organic matter (by direct determination)	0.97%
Nitrogen	0.03%
Phosphoric acid	0.20%
Potash	1.15%
Lime	0.60%

The remarks made on the sample of *murmad* soil, whose analysis has already been given, apply here equally or to an even greater extent.

The greater part of the village land, as is the case with most of the valley villages in this part of the Deccan, is composed of black soil. This material, variously called black cotton soil, or *regur*, derived from the finer portions of decayed trap rock as carried by water to lower levels, is not by any means always similar. Where the finest material and clay predominate it forms one of the most clayey soils in the world, contracting enormously when dry and forming masses as hard as iron, and consisting of a slimy jelly-like mass when saturated with water. Where the clay is not present in this amount, the special characters of the soil are exhibited to a smaller degree, but they are not dissimilar in kind. The heavier and more clayey black soils are characteristic of the eastern part of the Deccan (as would be expected) for there the slopes are less steep, the water, carrying alluvium, has had further to run, and hence the materials deposited are of a finer texture. As one proceeds to the west, the soils, though still black and possessing the characters above described in a measure, are less heavy and are usually styled 'medium black soil' or 'light black soil,' according to the amount of clay which they contain, or rather to the force (in bullocks) required to plough the land.

The greater part of the village-cultivated area is occupied by 'medium black soil,' that so classed being 691 acres out of a total cultivable area of 1,006 acres. It occupies all the centre of the village area. Its depth varies, as has already been explained and as will be seen from the sections across the area, becoming shallower near the river, and also toward the higher land on the outskirts of the village. Near the river the depth is, in fact, only one foot over much of the area, while over the greater part of the centre of the village it lies between this and five feet.

Where the soil is deep there is very little difference between the soil and subsoil in texture or in colour. Below the subsoil *murum* is invariably found, and below this the hard rock from which it is derived.

This medium black soil cracks deeply during the dry weather. Over most of the village a vast ramification of cracks will be found, ranging up to two to three inches wide, and going down in some cases at least to three feet deep.

The character of the black soil can be well seen from the following figures of analysis of the soil and subsoil in a typical case:—

PHYSICAL ANALYSIS.

		Soil (0 to 9" deep) %	Subsoil (9" to 18" deep) %
Coarse Sand and Gravel ..	(Over .16 mm in diameter)	6.7	5.8
Fine Sand ..	(.07 mm to .16 mm ,, ..	8.1	7.7
Coarse Silt ..	(.03 mm to .07 mm ,, ..	8.4	7.5
Medium Silt ..	(.01 mm to .03 mm ,, ..	10.7	13.6
Fine Silt ..	(.008mm to .01 mm ,, ..	61.2	59.7
Finest Silt and Clay	(less than .008 mm ,, ..	4.8	5.7

CHEMICAL ANALYSIS.

	Soil (0 to 9" deep) %	Subsoil (9" to 18" deep) %
Sand and insoluble Silicates..	63. 8	65. 7
Loss on ignition	19. 2	20. 6
Organic matter (by direct determination)..	2.38	(not determined.)

Nitrogen	0.06	0.05
Phosphoric acid	0.23	0.42
Potash	1. 6	0. 8
Lime	1. 9	1. 4

These figures are exceedingly striking and illustrate in a very effective manner the characteristics of the black soil not only of the village of Pimpla Soudagar, but also of a large part of the medium black soil areas of the Deccan. In the first place the exceeding similarity between the soil and subsoil is very marked. This, which is particularly characteristic of all semi-arid regions, is perhaps particularly so of the black soil areas of the Deccan.

As regards the size of the particles, the most prominent feature is the very small quantity of what can be classed as clay on account of its fineness, in a soil so markedly clayey as this black soil. It is probable that in a soil like this a very small amount of genuine colloidal clay is capable of giving its character to any soil in which fairly fine particles predominate. We know of no soil in which this character is so emphasised as in the Deccan black soil; we imagine that the fine silt here must be also in a very highly hydrolysed and in a semi-colloidal condition, and if this is the case the high percentage of combined water (see below) would be understood and also the great retentiveness of the soil for water.

The very high percentage of loss by ignition of the dried soil is also a very characteristic feature of black soil, and is due (as the figures given above illustrate) to the presence of much combined water and not to a large quantity of organic matter. The organic matter in fact in these soils is usually very small, and these samples are no exception. The origin of the black colour is not entirely known in spite of many inquiries.* It seems in part due to finely divided magnetic

* The latest of these is recorded in Annett. Mem. Dept. Agric. Ind. (Chem. Ser. Vol. I, No. 9 (1910) and by Harrison and Sivan. Mem. Dept. Agric. Ind. (Chem. Ser.), Vol. II, No. 5 (1912).

oxide of iron, but there are certainly other compounds which share in causing it. One thing is certain. It is not due to anything but a minor extent to organic matter, and, in fact, the black soils of the Deccan are remarkably deficient in humus, and hence in nitrogen. The deficiency in organic matter and nitrogen is, perhaps, the most strongly marked feature in the chemical analysis of Deccan soils. They are rich otherwise. The total and available phosphoric acid appear usually to be considerable, though they often respond to phosphatic manures though not much to potash manures. The lime is usually, if not always, in excess. But they contain, as a rule, only a small quantity of humus, and they respond very quickly to nitrogenous manures, provided the water in the soil is maintained sufficiently high in amount.

The water content represents, in fact, the limiting factor in the soils of the Deccan. If the water can be guaranteed, it pays to manure heavily with organic and nitrogenous manures, and also in many cases with phosphatic manures ; if not, and this is frequently the case, it does not pay to manure at all. The value of any particular soil in the Deccan depends primarily (1) on its retentiveness and (2) on its depth. The former is measured in a considerable measure by its clayey character. The latter is essentially important because the subsoil is usually either rock, or a hungry, highly porous, material like *murum* which may be of advantage as a source of water for large perennial plants, but is of little use for annual crops.

The primary importance of these two factors was recognised by Wingate's survey of 1835 and its later developments on which the whole land revenue system of the Deccan essentially depends. First we have a division of the land on a basis of its retentiveness, and along with this a further division on the basis of its depth. In fact, in the scheme put forward in 1847,* as a result of much experience by Wingate

* Letter to Government, dated August 2 1847.

and his coadjutors, a table for the classification of soils was given, and this classification was approved by the Government of Bombay* and has since remained the basis of the land revenue system in the western Presidency. The table was as follows :—

Class.	Relative value in class in annas or sixteenths of a rupee.	Soils of the 1st order — Of fine uniform texture, varying in colour from deep black to dark brown.	Soils of the 2nd order. — Of uniform but coarser texture than the preceding and lighter also in colour, which is generally red.	Soils of the 3rd order. — Of coarse, gravelly or loose friable texture and colour varying from light brown to grey.
		Depth in cubits.	Depth in cubits.	Depth in cubits.
1..	16	$1\frac{3}{4}$	..	..
2..	14	$1\frac{1}{2}$	$1\frac{3}{4}$	..
3..	12	$1\frac{1}{4}$	$1\frac{1}{2}$	..
4..	10	1	$1\frac{1}{4}$	..
5..	8	$\frac{3}{4}$	1	..
6..	6	$\frac{1}{2}$	$\frac{3}{4}$	1
7..	$4\frac{1}{2}$	$\frac{1}{4}$	$\frac{1}{2}$	$\frac{3}{4}$
8..	3	..	$\frac{1}{4}$	$\frac{1}{2}$
9..	2	..	..	$\frac{1}{4}$

Where by virtue of position or other factors the land is worth more than the class to which it would be assigned, an amount is added to bring its class to a higher position than its characters alone would warrant. We may thus have land which is worth more than 16 annas, that is to say, worth more than the maximum value by classification.

In this village the Government assessment revenue for land classed as 16 annas is at present Rs. 2/8/- per acre. From this the value of the rest can be easily calculated. The area to which various values are assigned is as follows :—

* See their letter dated September 22, 1848.

18 annas	6 acres.
17 annas	26 acres.
16 annas	11 acres.
15 annas	121 acres.
14 annas	168 acres.
13 annas ..	55 acres.
12 annas	64 acres.
11 annas	67 acres.
10 annas	106 acres.
9 annas	92 acres.
8 annas	69 acres.
7 annas	38 acres.
6 annas	32 acres.
5 annas	91 acres.
4 annas	74 acres.

If this be summarised we may express the revenue classification of the soils thus :—

Above 12 annas, or soil considered to be of above average value	387 acres.
8 to 12 annas, or soil of medium value ..	398 acres.
Under 8 annas, or inferior soil	235 acres.

It is interesting to compare these figures with those we have obtained from an examination of the soils, with reference only to their physical characters, which gave as follows :—

(1) Medium black soil	691
(2) Light black soil	166
(3) *Murmad* soil	56
(4) Yellow soil	112
	1,025*

* This includes 15 acres of land so bad as to be unassessed (*pot kharab*) and 4 acres of public land reserved for grazing.

Of these, Nos. 1 and 2 probably correspond with a revenue classification of not less than 8 annas, while Nos. 3 and 4 would be below this valuation.

These soil conditions represent a typical state of affairs in a large part of the western Deccan. The improvement of the *murmad* soil and the yellow soil shows so little prospect of profit that it is rarely undertaken anywhere, except where by the building of embankments a large amount of silt from the higher and still poorer lands can be caught, and the depth increased. Apart from this they yield a doubtful crop of *bajri* or other crop capable of standing considerable dryness of the soil, during the rains, and beyond such a crop cattle may find a little grazing among the stubbles for the rest of the year. In Pimpla Soudagar embanking has practically not been done at all, and very little is perhaps possible, and the light and uncertain *kharif* or rains crops are all that this land furnishes.

On the other hand, the retentive black soil yields a variable crop in both the *kharif* and *rabi* seasons, varying in character and in quantity with its depth. Its development beyond this point depends on the possibility of the supply of irrigation water whether from the river or from wells. This leads us to a consideration of the water which is available for the purpose and how it is used.

C.—Waters of the Village.

First let us consider the water of the river. This is not used at all for irrigation in Pimpla Soudagar, though it is hard to see why this has not been done. It is, however, the source of the drinking water, is the place where the cattle are watered, and is intensely important in the economy of the village. It represents a typical surface water in the Deccan, running off as it does either directly from the surface of the higher lands, or from below the superficial layers of the soil, and being retained into what is really a natural reservoir by the ridge of rocks below the village. The actual water running in the river in the hot weather is extremely small, but there is always enough retained in the reach before the village to carry the village through the hot season.

During the rains and for a considerable period afterwards, there is water in the two large *nalas* which run into the river in the village. These are able to affect the composition of the water in the river to a great extent at this time of the year. As being purely surface waters from a much more limited area they contain much less soluble salts than the river water itself. This effect disappears by November in each year when the *nalas* dry up.

To illustrate the character of these river waters, we have determined the quantity of solid matter and the nature of the salts in samples drawn from the river above and below the mouth of the chief *nala* near the *gaothan* at intervals of two months (more or less) throughout the year. The details of the analyses are shown in Appendix A, but we may point out certain features in connection with them here.

The total soluble matter is very small—ranging from sixteen parts per 100,000 at the point below where the *nala* joins it at the height of the rains in August, to forty parts per 100,000 above the *nala* mouth in October. Even the sample containing the most solid matter was very soft,—as is indeed generally the case with river and *nala* waters in the Deccan unless they are fed by waters which have percolated for considerable distances. Except at the height of the rains and when much diluted with the purely surface water brought down by the *nalas*, the composition is very constant, and seems much less affected by the season than might have been expected.

The actual salts contained in the water are quite characteristic of subsoil semi-superficial waters in the Deccan trap areas. Carbonates predominate in them, while the amount of sulphates and chlorides is small. The waters are often alkaline, and when not actually alkaline contain alkaline bicarbonates. The large amount of magnesium salts in proportion to those of calcium is characteristic of all Deccan trap waters, even the most superficial. Unless contaminated by refuse from this village or those above it, such a water would be an admirable drinking water, and is esteemed as such.

The character of the wells and well waters in the village has, perhaps, more interest. In Pimpla they are very few, but their position, the depth of the water in them from the surface of the ground, the direction from which the water flows into them, and the character of the water itself are all worth study as typical of well conditions in the Deccan. All the wells are old, beyond the memory of the present generation, and no new wells have been dug for many years.

All the wells of the village, which number twelve (though as one is derelict, our examination is really only of eleven) lie on three main lines. The first is in the basin of the *nala* to the west of the *gaothan* and includes six wells : the second line is on the higher land which lies between the two large *nalas* of the village and includes only two wells, but one of these is among the best in the village; while the third is in the basin of the *nala* to the east of the *gaothan* and includes four more wells.

Before dealing with each of these groups separately, we will take some general considerations which apply to them all.

(1) In all cases, it seems as if the well sinking has tapped not a generalised underground water supply, but water running in one or more fissures. This is most clearly indicated by the fact that the water which runs into the wells always does so from one side and never from all round and under the bottom. It usually appears to come from a horizontal fissure.

(2) In nearly all cases the water which is obtained appears to be running from south to north, that is to say, towards the river. The wells appear to intercept water which is running to join streams which, either above or below ground, follow the line of the river. This is important, for it suggests that there is little more chance of getting water near the river than further

away. Many people have imagined that the wells in a Deccan village are served with water from the river or the underground streams accompanying it: this is certainly not the case in the village under present consideration.

(3) The depth of the water in the wells gets greater as they are further from the river. That is to say, the slope of the horizontal fissures (in which most of the water runs) towards the river is less than the slope of the surface of the ground. This is to be expected, but the observations certainly confirm it.

(4) All the wells, except those numbered 2 and 3 in the following list, only give enough water to supply one *mhot* * during the greater part of the year. In these two cases the supply for part of the year is sufficient for two *mhots.*

The three groups of wells indicated above may now be described.

Group I.—These follow more or less the line of the western *nala* though they are often at some distance from it. We do not, except incidentally, give the depth of water from the surface of the ground as this will vary with the level of the site, and the wells cannot be easily compared with one another, but instead we have indicated the volume of water in the several wells presuming the wells are cylindrical. This is probably not far from the mark with *pucca* wells, but is not very accurate with *kachha* ones.

Well No. 1 (Survey No. 176) lies at a distance of almost exactly 1,000 feet from the river, and six hundred feet to the west of the *nala.* The ground slopes towards both the *nala* and the river from this point. It is a *pucca* well, and has a fairly constant supply of water.

Well No. 2 (Survey No. 180) lies 1,400 feet from the river and close by the side of the *nala.* It is also a *pucca* well.

* A *mhot* is the large leather bag by which water is drawn up from a well. It usually contains about thirty gallons, and in full work at the depth of these wells can be filled and drawn up about once a minute. In a day of eight hours' work, one *mhot* means here a daily supply of about 14,000 to 15,000 gallons a day.

The supply of water (see below) is not nearly so constant as in well No. 1. The water enters it from a fissure on the south of the well, it is hence running direct to the main river. It supplies sufficient water for two *mhots* during a considerable part of the year.

Well No. 3 (Survey No. 150) lies about the same distance from the river as the last and four hundred feet to the east of the *nala*. It lies on a level patch partially down the slope to the *nala*. It is a *pucca* well. The water flows into it from the south and is hence running to the main river. It supplies sufficient water for two *mhots* during a considerable part of the year.

Well No. 4 (Survey No. 159). This well is about one hundred feet from one branch of the western *nala*, and about 1,900 feet from the river. It lies on the same level patch as the last, partially down the slope leading to the *nala*. It is *pucca*, and the water enters it from a south or slightly south south-east direction.

Well No. 5 (Survey No. 136). This is a big *pucca* well near to the smaller branch of the western *nala*, which by this time has become a small dry stream bed during the greater part of the year. It is about 2,350 feet from the river in a direct line.

Well No. 6 (Survey No. 124). This well lies in the basin of the larger branch of the western *nala* and about two hundred feet from it. It lies 3,750 feet from the main river. It is *pucca*.

The depth of the water from the surfaces in some of these wells at different times of the year is as follows :—

		March 21st, 1914.		May 30th, 1914.
Well No. 3	..	6 feet	..	9 feet
Well No. 4	..	7 feet	..	10 feet
Well No. 5	..	10 feet	..	13 feet
Well No. 6	..	20 feet	..	32 feet

The alteration in the amount of the water in the wells at different times of the year is a better indication of the effect of season than the depth from the surface, and for each well is as follows. The measurements were taken in the morning and so weie not influenced appreciably by the water with drawn.

Well No. 1. (Capacity of well—54,150 gallons.)

		Volume of water : Gallons.	Percentage of volume in August.
August 1914	.. ..	36,122	100.0 per cent.
October 1914	.. ..	29,089	80.6 per cent.
January 1914	.. ..	24,046	66.8 per cent.
March 1914	.. ..	21,380	59.4 per cent.
May 1914	.. ..	16,378	45.5 per cent.

Well No. 2. (Capacity of well—31,750 gallons).

		Volume of water : Gallons.	Percentage of volume in August.
August 1914	.. ..	28,917	100.0 per cent.
October 1914	.. ..	26,082	89.0 per cent.
January 1914	.. ..	23,247	80.2 per cent.
March 1914	.. ..	17,011	58.7 per cent.
May 1914	.. ..	5,670	19.6 per cent.

Well No. 3. (Capacity of well—16,582 gallons).

		Volume of water : Gallons.	Percentage of volume in August.
August 1914	(well full)	16,582	100.0 per cent.
October 1914	.. ..	14,028	84.5 per cent.
January 1914	.. ..	12,983	78.2 per cent.
March 1914	.. ..	11,607	70.0 per cent.
May 1914	.. ..	4,521	27.2 per cent.

Well No. 4. (Capacity of well—24,135 gallons).

	Volume of water : Gallons.	Percentage of volume in August.
August 1914	23,688	100.0 per cent.
October 1914	22,347	94.3 per cent.
January 1914	19,665	83.0 per cent.
March 1914	17,633	74.4 per cent.
May 1914	6,034	25.5 per cent.

Well No. 5. (Capacity of well—52,449 gallons).

	Volume of water : Gallons	Percentage of volume in August.
August 1914	48,801	100.0 per cent.
October 1914	44,080	90.3 per cent.
January 1914	34,671	71.0 per cent.
March 1914	29,075	59.5 per cent.
May 1914	22,416	45.9 per cent.

Well No. 6. (Capacity of well—47,869 gallons).

	Volume of water : Gallons.	Percentage of volume in August.
August 1914	44,100	100.0 per cent.
October 1914	42,347	96.0 per cent.
January 1914	30,373	68.9 per cent.
March 1914	24,532	55.6 per cent.
May 1914	10,805	24.5 per cent.

The figures here quoted seem to indicate in a conclusive manner :—

(1) That the source of water is not identical in all cases or, in other words, that the wells tap independent fissures.

(2) That the sources are of differing degrees of permanence, or in other words, that the range of supply differs in the different wells.

(3) That even in the most superficial of these wells the water available is nearly sixty per cent. of the August supply until March in an average year, but that in the more superficial supplies it falls rapidly after this time.

(4) That in this group of wells two types can be noted, one represented by Nos. 1 and 5 in which the hot weather supply (May) is nearly equal to fifty per cent. of the August supply, the other represented by Nos. 2, 3, 4 and 6 in which the hot weather supply is on the average less than a quarter of the August supply.

Similar conclusions could probably be drawn about the superficial supplies of rock water in most groups of wells in the Deccan. We will see the results which a similar treatment of the other two groups of wells will give.

Group II.—The wells in this group are only two, but are interesting as lying on the level higher land between the basins of the two large *nalas* in the village. One of these (that in Survey No. 4) is not used and is filled up. It is a great pity that this is the case, as its examination would have been of great interest. It is, however, too near to the village and especially to the *mahar wada* (or quarter of the village for the low caste classes) to be used for cultivation, and is not needed for drinking as the river is so near.

The other well in Survey No. 71 is of great interest. It is near the *gaothan*, is not used for crops, but is surrounded by trees, is not *pucca* built, as owing to the rocky character of the situation this is not needed, and it is the largest well in the village area. It is less than 500 feet from the river and again the water enters it from the south, that is to say, from the side furthest from the river.

Data for this well, similar to those already given for those in Group I, are as follows :—

Well No. 7. (Total capacity of well—1,65,630 gallons).

		Volume of water: Gallons.	Percentage of volume in August.
August 1914	..	1,59,432	100.0 per cent.
October 1914	..	1,03,652	65.0 per cent.
January 1914	..	69,885	43.8 per cent.
March 1914	..	66,786	41.9 per cent.
May 1914	..	74,800	47.0 per cent.

It is evident that here we have a type of well different from either of those contained in Group I. There is certainly a semi-superficial supply which fills up the well in the rainy season. This disappears however soon after the rains are over, and then there is a practically constant supply from deeper sources, which presumably have a larger range of supply and which fill the well as much in the hot weather as during the months from November to March.

Group III.—The third group of wells is in the basin of the eastern *nala*. It comprises four wells which may be described as follows :—

Well No. 8 (Survey No. 27) lies at a distance of seven hundred feet from the river and almost the same distance from the *nala* itself. It has been dug on a nearly level stretch partially down the slope towards the *nala*. It is a *pucca* well, damaged however on one side, and vegetables as well as fruit trees have been and are grown on the water from it. The water enters from the south, and would appear to be running direct to the river.

Well No. 9 (Survey No. 31) lies 1,300 feet from the river and 800 feet from the western branch of the *nala*. The water in this likewise enters from the south. It is dug in another part of the same level stretch as Well No. 8 ; is *pucca* built, and is used for the growing of vegetables and fruit trees.

Well No. 10 (Survey No. 40) lies 4,000 feet from the river and 450 feet from the western branch of the *nala*. The water enters from the south and flows, as in other cases, in the direction of the river. The well is *pucca* and is used for irrigating *rabi* crops.

Well No. 11 (Survey No. 50) lies four hundred feet further from the river than the last, and in a similar position with regard to the *nala*. The water again enters from the south and flows towards the main river.

The alteration in the water contained in these four wells at different times of the year are as follows, the measurements being made similarly to those in the previous cases ;—

Well No. 8. (Capacity of well—27,286 gallons).

		Volume of water : Gallons.	Percentage of volume in August.
August 1914	..	27,134	100.0 per cent.
October 1914	..	20,356	75.1 per cent.
January 1914	..	9,961	37.0 per cent.
March 1914	..	4,331	16.0 per cent.
May 1914	..	346	1.3 per cent.

Well No. 9. (Capacity of well—49,018 gallons).

		Volume of water : Gallons.	Percentage of volume in August.
August 1914	..	41,145	100.0 per cent.
October 1914	..	35,515	86.4 per cent.
January 1914	..	24,470	59.5 per cent.
March 1914	..	22,197	54.0 per cent.
May 1914	..	18,948	46.1 per cent.

Well No. 10. (Capacity of well—61,300 gallons).

		Volume of water : Gallons.	Percentage of volume in August.
August 1914	..	60,941	100.0 per cent.
October 1914	..	46,434	76.2 per cent.
January 1914	..	38,437	63.1 per cent.
March 1914	..	30,122	49.5 per cent.
May 1914	..	22,713	37.3 per cent.

Well No. 11. (Capacity of well—86,946 gallons).

		Volume of water : Gallons.	Percentage of volume in August.
August 1914	..	84,197	100.0 per cent.
October 1914	..	76,137	90.4 per cent.
January 1914	..	50,899	60.4 per cent.
March 1914	..	40,536	48.1 per cent.
May 1914	..	31,703	37.6 per cent.

The general conclusions with regard to these wells are similar to those for Group I. We have here, however, in Well No. 8 a type of exceedingly local fissure water, which fails almost if not altogether in the hot weather. The other three correspond in type to well Nos. 1 and 5 in the basin of the western *nala*.

Taking the village as a whole we have therefore four types of wells.

(1) That represented by Well No. 7 in the area between the two *nalas* which has an excess of local water for two or three months in the rains, but is constant for the rest of the year.

(2) That represented by Wells Nos. 1 and 5 in Group I, and by Wells Nos. 9, 10 and 11 in Group III in which the hot weather supply is nearly equal to half the August supply.

(3) That represented by Wells Nos. 2, 3, 4 and 6 in Group I, in which the hot weather supply is on the average less than a quarter of the August supply.

(4) That represented by Well No. 8 where the supply disappears almost entirely in the hot weather.

We are justified in regarding these as wells drawing their supplies from fissures at different depths, or from gradually decreasing areas of trap rock, as one proceeds from the type No. 1 to type No. 4. We hope in a later paper to consider what effect this change of depth or change of area of supply has on the composition of the water of the wells. At present we can class the water in all of them as a fairly soft semi-superficial trap water, containing from 12 to 60 parts per 100,000 of solid matter. The dominant salts are carbonates, the largest proportion of these being always the calcium and magnesium salts. There is often, however, sodium carbonate and sodium bicarbonate present, and one can easily see that many of them in the absence of a large excess of lime and magnesia in the soil might become decidedly alkaline, as indeed happens fairly frequently with Deccan well waters. The amount of chlorides and sulphates is small,—sometimes, in fact, sulphates are entirely absent. On the whole, except in the most superficial supplies the total amount of salts present in the soil varies very little, far less than one would anticipate in a place where the water supply is so entirely restricted to one season.

All the waters are suitable for irrigation, and can be used without danger, and the water supply is sufficient in most of them for *rabi* or cold weather crops, and in five or six of them for crops which need a moderate amount of water in the hot weather. Most of the wells are not, however, largely used for irrigation, and this is attributed by the people to the following causes :—

(1) Owing to the subdivision of land (see later) the wells usually belong to several co-sharers in what was originally one holding. None of these cares to undertake the expense of maintaining the well, and as a result it is often in a bad condition, with appliances broken down, and cannot be easily used.

(2) Owing to the actual supply being small, it is not considered to be a paying proposition to keep the necessary bullocks, etc., for the irrigation of the limited area which could be irrigated.

D.—Drainage of the Village.

The irregularity of the surface of the land combined with the very heavy rainfall during a short period of the year and complete drought during the remainder renders the question of the drainage away of the surface water, without leading to a loss of surface soil, a matter of very great importance in a Deccan village. In the consideration of this question Pimpla Soudagar may be considered as absolutely a typical village. The irregularity of its surface is very great, though there is a comparatively large area which can be classed as level, or nearly so. Such land amounts to about 881 acres, or 82·7 per cent. of the total village area.

The drainage of the village takes place in three directions. Chiefly along the banks of the Pawana river there is a small area which tends to be badly cut up, which drains directly into that river. Where this is the case, unless special precautions are taken by the landholders, gullies sometimes almost amounting to miniature ravines, tend to be formed by the drainage water, for the difference in level between the land and the river is very great. Much of the village is, however, protected from such deep cutting and gullying of the land by the ridge of rock near the river bank of which we have previously spoken and on which the *gaothan* or village site stands.

This deep gullying near the banks of a river is, however one of the characteristic features of almost every river valley in the Deccan. It can be seen everywhere, and the deeper and richer the land the more serious is the damage unless special precautions are taken and embankments made. In the village at present very few embankments exist except in the south-east corner, and there is only one protecting the land on the banks of the river from washing and gullying. This, however, built a good many years ago by one of the inamdars, has been of great service in preventing damage by the western *nala* near the mouth of which it was constructed.

The remainder of the land drains pretty directly into one or other of the large *nalas*, or one of their branches. The gullying of which we have spoken in the case of the land on the banks of the river is much more marked in the basins of the two *nalas* and if it were not that in this village much of the lands is of a fairly level character, the damage would have been much worse than it is. As a matter of fact, in only about six or seven instances has the damage been such as to make a field useless. In this part of the Deccan and, in fact, in the Deccan generally, a very slight slope on a field, even such a slope as can hardly be noticed, is enough to cause washing and gullying to such an extent as to affect materially the value of the field so far as depth of soil is concerned. In the present case, a small number of fields have been neglected in this matter and they are now practically useless. We estimate that the conversion of useful into useless area on this account has only affected seriously at present an area of 10 acres or nearly one per cent. of the village area.

So far, however, in this village the embanking has not attempted more than the preservation of a few individual fields which are already useful. There had been no attempt to increase the actually useful areas by arranging for the deposition of silt from the higher areas on the lower but still rocky or *mal* land. This operation, which has been done with very great success in some places in the Deccan, has no illustration in the village now under discussion.

The limit of the effort in this village has been in a few cases to level and embank the fields which are actually nearly level, and to divert the streams of water, which would be likely to damage the fields, either on to someone else's property or on to the roads and footpaths in the village and so into the *nalas* themselves. When a footpath becomes in this way the course of a drainage stream, it usually deepens very quickly until a layer of either rock or very hard *murum* is reached, which it cannot wash away at all easily. We cannot insist too much in attempting to describe a typical village in the Deccan on the extraordinary amount of erosion which occurs, attributable to the generally non-level character of the land, to the small amount of penetration which the water is able to get unless the land is very well prepared before the coming of the rain, and lastly, to the violence of the rain when it does come, often at the rate of an inch per hour for several hours after a drought which has lasted seven or eight months.

3

CHAPTER III.

THE LAND AND ITS DIVISIONS, AND THE HOLDINGS.

IT is not our intention to try and describe in the present paper the system of land tenure which is in vogue in the Deccan at the present time. This has been done many times and in no case more clearly than in Keatinge's " Rural Economy of the Bombay Deccan "* previously referred to. In order to make, however, our description of how the land is held intelligible, we may quote a passage from the latter work where the whole question is summarised.

" The law which defines the present system of land tenure and assessment is embodied in the Bombay Land Revenue Code (Bombay Act V of 1879). The *mirasi* and *upri* tenures of olden days have been merged into a uniform tenure as the survey or occupancy tenure. Full occupancy tenure is a heritable and transferable property, which allows the occupant to hold the land in perpetuity and to cultivate it himself or to lease it to others for cultivation, subject to the payment of land revenue. The land revenue is a tax which has some of the characteristics of rent, and varies from field to field according to the fertility of the soil and other natural advantages. The tenure is known as *ryotwari*: that is to say, each landholder holds his land direct from Government. It reproduces in the main the features of the old *mirasi* tenure, but differs from it in four respects, *viz.* :—

(1) " The occupant has the right to sell or otherwise alienate his land without the permission of Government.

(2) Failure to pay the assessment renders the occupancy liable to forfeiture.

* Pages 20 and 21.

(3) The assessment is liable to revision every thirty years.

(4) A guarantee is given that no additional taxation will be levied on account of improvements made by the occupant."

Such is the modern system which may perhaps be considered a natural development of the land system in the Deccan in pre-British times. It presumes that the whole of the land revenue, in default of a definite grant to someone else, goes direct through the village officers to a representative of Government. "In default of a definite grant to someone else," we say, for it is rare that there is not some right to be satisfied from the village revenue, as represented by the land assessment. The various grants or *inams* which were made in the time of the rule of the Peshwas and in the early days of British rule form a very interesting study, and the present village forms an exceedingly good illustration of the condition of things in most Deccan villages to a greater or less extent. We have had the opportunity of looking over the records of the village, which date back in a fragmentary form to the year 1699, and a short account of the extent of alienation of revenue, of the character and size of the holdings, of the extent to which the revenue was collected, and of cognate matters, translated into modern terms and measures will enable us to compare modern conditions with those which have prevailed in the past.

A.—Village Inams.

The first record of the village conditions that we have been able to find is, as already stated, that for 1699-1700. At that time the village* area was practically as it is at present, namely, 1,065 acres. The total assessment is not recorded, but 198 acres were *inam* land, that is to say, land the revenue

* In interpreting the records we have taken the following measurements :—

1 *takka*=48 *rukka*, 1 *rukka*=$4\frac{2}{3}$ acres, 1 *takka*=224 acres. These are calculated from our knowledge of the village area both formerly and at present.

from which was granted to others than the Government. These were as follows :—

(1) For the maintenance of the temple at Chinchvad —84 acres.
(2) For Mahabai—84 acres.
(3) For Mokaddam, a village officer—42 acres.
(4) For Padewar—28 acres.

The nature of the second and fourth of these items is doubtful, though it seems practically certain that the fourth is the land reserved for the *mahars** of the village. The second, on the other hand, is absolutely uncertain, though we are inclined to suggest that it represents the *inam* afterwards found in the name of the Purandhare family of Poona. The first and the third are of greater interest.

The devotion of land to the maintenance of temples is one of the oldest forms of *inam* in the Deccan. Of the origin of the present one we have not got hold of any record, and it remains to this day. The temple of Chinchvad to which it is devoted is a well-known one and somewhat famous in the neighbourhood. Many of the villages have similar *inams*.

The third is interesting, and indicates the method adopted by the Maratha Government of paying the village officers. For this purpose the revenue of land was alienated to them. At this time apparently one man received the lot. He was the village *patel*, and there is no record of the amount being shared by any other officer. The arrangement continued until after British rule was established, but as time went on, the number of village and local officers who had the land revenue from a definite area of land granted to them, tended (as we shall see) to increase. At this date the assessment of 814 acres was, apparently, paid to the Government of that day.

Seventy-one years later (1770-71) we come to a period when the records are more complete and detailed. With a

* For the duties and status of the village *mahars* see Chapter VI.

village area similar to that in 1700, the land whose revenue was alienated had risen to 266 acres, or an increase of twenty-eight acres.

The *inams* at this date were :—

(1)	For temples at Chinchvad ..	..84 acres.
(2)	For village *Patel*	..42 acres.
(3)	For village *Mahars*	..28 acres.
(4)	For Purandhare Bhat of Poona ..	..84 acres.
(5)	For Narhar Bhat of Pandharpur (Special *inam*).	..28 acres.

Items (1) and (2) are as they were seventy years before. Item (3) also probably remains identical, and represents the land whose revenue was payable to this class of village servants, or which they were allowed to cultivate. We shall have more to say about this later on. The fourth is possibly the same as that marked to " Mahabai " in the previous record, and the last is a new and definite grant by the ruling authority of the day to some of his servants in the manner favoured by the Maratha rulers always.

Nine years later (1779-80) the *inam* land remains the same except that item No. (5) temporarily drops out, and the actual recipient of No. (4) is a different man of the same family. The village *patel's* share is divided among two persons. Another change, however, occurs in the records for 1797-98, when the *inams* are as follows :—

(1)	For temple at Chinchvad	..84 acres.
(2)	For village *Patel*	..42 acres.
(3)	For village *Mahars*	..28 acres.
(4)	For Damodar Bhat Purandhare ..	..84 acres.
(5)	For Narhar Bhat, Pandharpur ..	..28 acres.
(6)	For village *Kulkarni*	..12 acres.

The second special *inam* (5) now reappears, and a new *inam* for a second village officer the *Kulkarni* or village clerk and accountant appears for the first time. This area of *inam* land, and the people to which it was devoted, remain the same right up to the British conquest in 1817-18.

To continue the history of the village *inams*. In 1819 a new factor was introduced, in the grant of the whole Government revenues from this village to one man, Rango Pandit Khole, who had assisted in the British occupation. The actual details with regard to this grant, as recorded by the *Inam* Commission in 1856 were as follows, the account being taken from a letter from Captain Briggs, Political Agent in Khandesh, dated December 7th, 1818.*

"I consider it a duty I owe to the individuals who have "afforded me such zealous assistance, to bring their merits "particularly to your notice with a hope that you will be "disposed to recommend to Government some permanent "reward for their services..........Rungo Pandit, a res- "pectable Brahmin of Poona, with whom I had some "acquaintance while there: he was detailed at the same "time with 300 auxiliary horse and an advance of 5,000 rupees "to occupy the Gungterry : his activity and personal acquain- "tance with many of the *killadars* of the Forts, as well as a "considerable share of address, enabled him to occupy almost "without resistance all the plain................ I beg "to propose that they should each have grants of such villages "in the vicinity of their houses as they themselves might "select, to descend in one generation to their children and "afterwards to be held by their posterity in perpetuity at "an assessment equal to half the present rate........I beg "leave to suggest the following value of the village for Rango "Pandit, a village whose Tunkhah shall not exceed "2,000 rupees."

The proposal was sanctioned in January 1819 by the Governor-General, and the village of Pimpla Soudagar was

* A copy of the whole record and decision on the subject by the *Inam* Commission is given in the Appendix.

selected. The grant was converted by the *Inam* commission to a definite money grant in 1856 based on the nett revenue of the village in 1818-19, namely, Rs. 910. This amount was to be paid to the family of Rango Pandit Khole until the next generation after him was extinct, and thereafter the half of this (Rs. 455) to his family in perpetuity. It is, of course, still being paid, and is now divided between six representatives of the family.

Previous to this final settlement by the *Inam* commission the amount actually paid to the inamdar varied. As already stated it was Rs. 910 in 1818-19 : in 1829-30 it was Rs. 705 : in 1840-41 it was Rs. 523-14-6. By the last date, a large part of the revenue of the *inam* had been mortgaged by the grantee, and he only actually received Rs. 211 out of the amount.

Of the older *inams* all still remain, though they are of reduced area and though only parts of the assessment is now given up to the holders. The village *patil* and *kulkarni* are now, however, regular paid officers of Government, and so the reason for the continuance of the *inams* in their original form may perhaps have disappeared.

At the present time these older *inam* lands are divided up no less than forty shares. The average proportion of the total assessment of the land, as calculated by the ordinary Government survey methods, which is payable to Government is almost exactly thirty-five per cent. The proportion varies very widely, however, in different cases.

B.—Land Revenue from the Village.

The next question is as to what has been the actual value of this land assessment revenue at different periods. Our notes on this point do not go so far back as they do with regard to the *inams*, but they take us at any rate to 1770-71.

At this date (1770-71) there were 798 acres whose revenue, less expenses, was payable to Government. The gross revenue from this actually obtained was Rs. 801, or slightly more than Re. 1-0-0 per acre, cultivated and uncultivated, including village site, roads and *nalas*. Expenses amounted to Rs. 74, being Rs. 24 for village servants, Rs. 30 for annual expenses of collection, and Rs. 20 paid in addition to one of the inamdars, Narhar Bhat Purandhare, an explanation of which is not extant.

Twenty years later (1791-92) the actual gross revenue recovered had hardly changed, and amounted to Rs. 792-8-0, of which Rs. 780-8-0 was from ordinary assessed land, and Rs. 12 in some unexplained way from the *mahars*. The expenses had, however, very largely increased and now amounted to Rs. 202 instead of Rs. 74, so that the nett revenue receivable by the Government representative was much reduced and only amounted to Rs. 588-8. The items of this increased expenditure are interesting and are as follows :—

(1) To local Officers :—

(a) Deshmukh (1)	.. .. ..	Rs. 25
(b) Deshmukh (2)	.. .. ..	„ 8
(c) Deshpande	.. .. ..	„ 25
(d) Sar Patil	.. .. ..	„ 13
(e) Village Kulkarni	.. .. ..	„ 16
	Total ..	Rs. 87

(2) To actual expenses :—

(a) Government (सरकार बाब) ..	Rs.	19	8	0
(b) Festivities, visits, etc. ..	„	12	0	0
(c) A wandering group (१ झुंडा) of *Gosavis**	„	28	4	0

* We are not sure of the nature of this expense. Mr. Keatinge in a private note to us makes the following suggestion :—

"I do not know what were the circumstances in this case : but the Peshwas enrolled regiments of *gosavis* and in some cases special contributions were levied from villages to pay for them. I would suggest that it may have been so in this case and that the money levied may have been for the support of this irregular force and not for a wandering group of *Gosavis*."

(d) Minor charities	Rs.	3	0	0
(e) Gifts	„	24	8	0
(f) Spent on visits of Government Officers	„	4	3	0
(g) Sundry expenses	„	4	0	0
Total	Rs.	95	7	0

(3) Minor and unexpected expenses ..	Rs.	21	7	0

This illustrates in a very striking manner the increase of leakage of revenue in the later part of the Peshwa's period. New local officials appear in the *deshmukhs* and *deshpandes* who levy a toll on the revenue of each village, while the *patil* and *kulkarni* think that they must have a share too, in addition to the revenue of their *inam* lands. The other expenditure, specified and unexpected, increases, and it might seem that items (2) (a), (b), (c), (f), and much of (g), as well as much of (3) were possibly *solatia* to local officials of one sort or another.

At this time, however, we are at the beginning of the anarchy which occurred in the last few years of the Peshwa's rule, and its effect is well illustrated by the records for 1797-98. The amount of assessment received was Rs. 1,087-2-0. Out of this amount, larger than had ever been obtained before, only Rs. 390 reached the Government treasury. It was the time of the transit of armies, more or less rebellious, through the country, levying exactions as they went. We do not know how much the village people themselves paid, but we can trace the loss to the Government revenue. Some items of expenditure were as follows. We need hardly give a complete list :—

(1) Levied by the army of Shinde and Holkar	Rs.	178	13	6
(2) Feast to Officers of do. ..	„	14	0	0
(3) Present to messenger who brought .. news of Bajirao Peshwa's marriage ..	„	20	0	0

(4) *Pagri* of condolence to Khanderao ..	Rs.	4	0	0
(5) To *Koli* who did not get his annual *baluta* (present of grain, etc.,) on account of a riot	,,	7	0	0

In 1811-12 conditions were evidently a little better so far as levies by invading armies were concerned, but the assessment was higher and more gross revenue was obtained. Out of Rs. 1,158 received, however, only Rs. 848 were received by the Government officer appointed for the purpose. The local expenses were hence Rs. 310 and the local leakage of revenue was hence greater than ever. In 1817-18, the year before British rule really made any changes, the assessment was again higher and produced Rs 1,226-8.

In 1829-30, the assessment which had been fixed at Rs. 10 per rukka ($4\frac{2}{3}$ acres) was lowered to Rs. 8 per rukka on account of scarcity, and produced Rs. 889 as gross revenue. The total expenses apart from the inamdar's portion (Rs. 703) amounted to Rs. 186-12. These figures are specially interesting as they represent the condition after the consolidation of British rule, and are comparable with those before 1817-18.

If we put together a summary of the position at various periods from 1770 to 1830, the revenue figures afford a very interesting indication of the state of the country, and the efficiency of the administration. They do not, we think, give any indication of the prosperity of the people, for it would appear that the increase or decrease of the assessed revenue depended not so much on the ability of the people to pay as on the amount which it was supposed might be obtained from them. We have, however, the following as a summary of the position at various dates :—

	1770-71	1791-92	1797-98	1811-12	1829-30
Total assessed revenue.. ..	Rs. 801	Rs. 792-8	Rs. 1,087-2	Rs. 1,158	Rs. 889
Expenses	,, 74	,, 202	,, 697-2	,, 310	,, 186
Nett revenue ..	,, 727	,, 590-8	,, 390	,, 848	,, 703

After this time we enter on the modern period, the time of regular settlements, and regular revenue returns. The actual figures of gross revenue at several dates were as follows :—

	1849-50	1886-87	1914-15
Total assessed revenue	Rs. 1,115	Rs. 1,128	Rs, 1,660

C.—Holdings in the Village.

So far we have dealt with the history of the alienated or *inam* holdings, and of the actual revenue obtained by the various Governments from the village. Now let us consider the size of the actual holdings and hence the number of landholders. It must be understood that the system has always been ryotwari, that is to say, that each individual landholder has direct relationship with the Government. The earliest records which give details as to holdings are those of 1771-72 where the number of actual holders of land (exclusive of the *inams*) was nineteen only, and their holdings were as follows :—

Number with more than 30 acres of land ..	12
Number with 20 to 30 acres of land	6
Number below 20 acres	1
Largest individual holding	74 acres.
Smallest individual holding	7 acres.
Average size of holding*	40 acres.

Of the total area of 787 acres, 278 were classed as *kharif* and 509 acres as *rabi* area.

By 1791-92 very considerable progress had been made in the reduction in the size of holdings. There were now thirty-five owners of land, and their holdings were as follows :—

* In getting this figure we have considered the area kept for public purposes (village site, etc.,) as identical throughout the period under consideration, and have omitted the *inam* lands from consideration.

Number with more than 30 acres of land ..	None.
Number with 20 to 30 acres of land	10
Number with 10 to 20 acres of land	14
Number with 5 to 10 acres of land	4
Number with less than 5 acres of land	7
Largest individual holding	28 acres.
Smallest individual holding	2⅓ acres
Average size of holding	21 acres.

Six years later (1797-98) the corresponding figures were as follows :—

Total number of landowning cultivators ..	28
Number with more than 30 acres of land ..	2
Number with 20 to 30 acres of land	9
Number with 10 to 20 acres of land	10
Number with 5 to 10 acres of land	7
Number with less than 5 acres of land	None.
Largest individual holding	56 acres.
Smallest individual holding	6 acres.
Average size of holding	26½ acres.

By 1811-12 the number of cultivators had again increased to 48, the largest individual holding was 44 acres, and the smallest 2⅓ acres. In 1817-18, immediately before the British occupation, the number had again decreased to 42 ; the largest individual holding was 35 acres, and the smallest 2⅓ acres as before. If one may connect the condition of the country with the number of holders, one might almost think that, under the Deccan system of family custom, the more peaceful the time the more the number of landholders, and the more disturbed the conditions, the smaller the number and hence the larger the holdings. Thus we have :—

	Number of landholders.	Average size of holding.
1771-72	19	40 acres.
1791-92	35	21 acres.

	Number of landholders.	Average size of holding.
1797-98	28	26½ acres.
1811-12	48	15½ acres.
1817-18	42	17½ acres.

Since the British occupation the number of landholding cultivators has become continually greater, and the size of the holding continually less. Thus we have :—

1829-30—

Total number of landholding cultivators ..	52
Average size of holding ..	14 acres.

1840-41—

Total number of landholding cultivators ..	54
Average size of holding ..	14 acres.

In all these cases we have, as already noted, taken no account of the land held under privileged or *inam* tenure, and, moreover, we have counted all land separately held as a separate holding. At the present time (1914-15) we are able to analyse the holdings more completely, and to include the *inam* land in consideration. If we do this we get figures as follows :—

Total number of holdings (including those of *inam* land and joint holdings.)	156
Total number of holdings, excluding joint holdings held by one of the joint holders	140
Total number of holdings, held under *inam* rights ..	40
Number of holders (including inamdars and joint holdings) with more than 40 acres	1
Number of holders (including inamdars and joint holdings) with 30 to 40 acres	1
Number of holders (including inamdars and joint holdings) with 20 to 30 acres	9

Number of holders (including inamdars and joint holdings) with 10 to 20 acres 18
Number of holders (including inamdars and joint holdings) with 5 to 10 acres 34
Number of holders (including inamdars and joint holdings) with 1 to 5 acres 71
Number of holders (including inamdars and joint holders) with less than 1 acre 22

It is evident from this that in the last sixty or seventy years the character of the land holdings has altogether changed. In the pre-British days, and in the early days of British rule the holdings were usually of a fair size, most frequently more than nine or ten acres, while individual holdings of less than two acres were hardly known. Now, the number of holdings is more than doubled, and eighty-one per cent. of these holdings are under ten acres in size, while no less than sixty per cent. are less than five acres.

We have no reason to suppose that the case of Pimpla Soudagar is anything but typical, and the above figures illustrate very clearly the extent to which subdivision is taking place with results which we will discuss later.

It is interesting to note that of these one hundred and fifty-six holdings, only twenty are held as joint property of several members of a family, or under thirteen per cent. of the whole. In view of the tendency to the retention of family property jointly under the Indian system it is interesting to find the small amount of such joint holdings which prevails in a typical village, such as that under consideration.

The excessive subdivision which has progressively increased during British rule is recognised as a very great evil. Keatinge has suggested that an economic holding of good dry land such as is most in this village in the western Deccan, and with an Indian *raiyat's* standard of life, would be about ten to fifteen acres. Even, therefore, if each holding were held in one block it is evident what a large proportion (81 per cent.) are below this size. It means, therefore, that by far the larger number

PLATE VII.
(To face Page 46.)

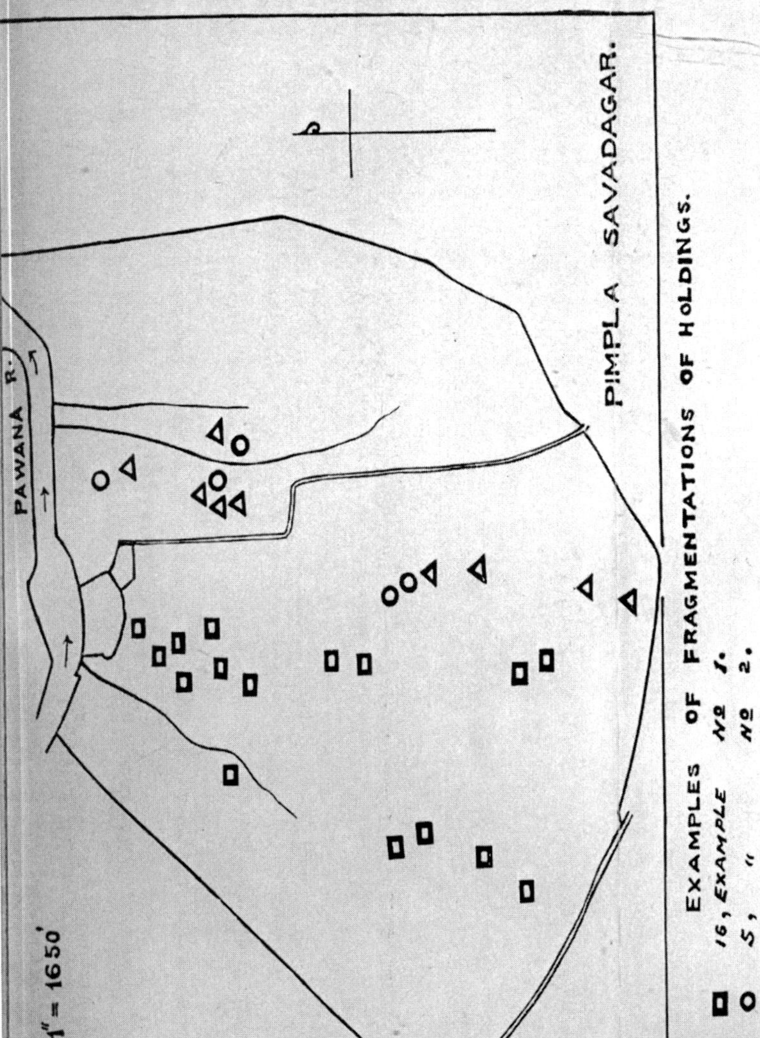

of holdings could not, under the most favourable circumstances, maintain their owners, but that they must rely on other occupations, either at home or away, to support themselves and their families, or else they must sublet their holdings. We shall see later that both these remedies are being adopted by the people.

The conditions are, however, not the most favourable, because there has been not only extreme subdivision, but also what Keatinge has termed "fragmentation," or what is known in French as *morcellement*. That is to say, that when under Hindu law landed property must be divided among the members of a family, the division is made by dividing each piece of land, and not by the various claimants taking the whole of the various sections of it. The evil result is very apparent in the village now under consideration.

Out of 156 landholders in the village only 28 hold all their property in a single survey number, and in a single piece. The actual condition is shown shortly in the following table :—

Holders of	Number of holders with this nnmber of plots.	Average area of holding.	Largest holding.	Largest plot.	Smallest holding.	Smallest plot.
		Acres.	Acres.	Acres.	Acres	Acres.
One plot ..	28	2.82	21.5	21.5	0.075	0.075
Two plots ..	31	2.96	22.3	18.1	0.7	0.075
Three plots ..	13	9.69	52.7	19.5	1.17	0. 05
Four plots ..	19	6.18	23.3	8.0	1.87	0.075
Five plots ..	19	4.73	10.1	7.1	2.07	0.075
Six plots ..	13	8.38	24.4	17.6	1.65	0.100
Seven plots ..	8	10.06	25.8	16.1	2.12	0.125
Eight plots ..	5	8.30	17.6	5.6	3.97	0.100
Nine plots ..	4	19.49	38.5	15.6	7.95	0.050
Ten plots ..	3	10.06	14.1	3.6	7.97	0.032
Eleven plots ..	5	13.07	26.6	5.1	7.22	0.100
Twelve plots ..	3	12.17	16.9	3.1	6.57	0.125
Fourteen plots ..	1	10.07	10.1	1.3	10.07	0.125
Sixteen plots ..	1	8.32	8.3	2.0	8.32	0.050
Seventeen plots..	1	9.55	9.5	2.0	9.5	0.125
Nineteen plots ..	1	15.02	15.0	2.2	15.02	0.050
Twenty plots ..	1	29.20	29.2	5.1	29.20	0.075

These figures indicate very clearly the extreme fragmentation of the land in the village. The 156 owners have between them no less than 718 separate plots. Of these the number of plots of various sizes is as follows :—

*Size of plots.**	*Number of plots of each size.*
Over 20 acres	1
10 to 20 acres	7
5 to 10 acres	21
3 to 5 acres	35
2 to 3 acres	67
1 to 2 acres	164
30 to 40 gunthas †	75
20 to 30 gunthas	136
15 to 20 gunthas	71
10 to 15 gunthas	57
5 to 10 gunthas	59
Below 5 gunthas	25

So far nothing definite has been done by public authority to stop this excessive fragmentation, which is an evil of far greater moment than that merely of great subdivision. It has, in fact, all the evils of very small holdings in that it prevents the use of machinery and labour-saving methods, and, on the other hand, of large holdings in that it hinders

* To get an absolutely clear idea of the situation, the following table arranged in a slightly different manner may be useful:—

Size of Plots.	*Number of plots of each size*
Over 10 acres	8
9 to 10 acres	0
8 to 9 acres	2
7 to 8 acres	8
6 to 7 acres	1
5 to 6 acres	8
4 to 5 acres	20
3 to 4 acres	17
2 to 3 acres	67
1 to 2 acres	164
Below 1 acre	428

† 1 guntha=one fortieth of an acre.

the adoption of really intensive cultivation by hand labour which is the great advantage of the small holder. We do not want to discuss here the methods by which public authorities might attempt to find a way out of the *impasse*, as they have attempted to do under the very similar difficulties which have occurred in several countries on the continent of Europe.

But the matter shows signs that it is, in part, settling itself by two processes, which are really part of one thing. The first of these is the abandonment of village life, though not of village land, by an increasing number of people, and the second the subletting of a large amount of the land by its holders.

The extent to which the landholders have left the village without relinquishing ownership is shown by the fact that only 90, or 64 per cent., of the total number now cultivate their holdings. The remainder, or 36 per cent., have become labourers either in the village or away from it at Kirkee or elsewhere and have ceased being cultivators in the ordinary sense.

D.—Areas held or taken for Cultivation.

A consequence of the extreme subdivision and fragmentation of the land which we have just discussed is subletting, and the fact that this is taking place to a considerable extent is evident. Our investigations show only 109 actual cultivators in the season of 1915 as against 156 landholders, or 140 landholders if joint holdings really held by one of the joint holders be excluded. We have then the introduction of a number of new cultivators who are not landholders, who now form 17 per cent. of the total number of actual cultivators, and some of whom deal with larger areas of land than most of the actual holders of land.

We had expected that these new non-landholding cultivators would be chiefly outsiders. This is not, however, the case. Practically all of them are members of the village who did not formerly cultivate land, but who had official connection with the village such as the village Mohammedan, the village barber, and so on, as well as some members of the leading cultivators' families who for some reason had no share in the land.

The relations between the size of the areas held by the various holders and the size of the areas cultivated by the various cultivators is shown in the following statement :—

	Holdings.		Areas cultivated by a single man.	
	Number. *	Percentage of total number. %	Number.	Percentage of total number. %
Above 40 acres ..	1	0.7	2	1.8
30 to 40 acres ..	2	1.4	2	1.8
20 to 30 acres ..	7	5.0	11	10.1
10 to 20 acres ..	14	10.0	10	9.2
5 to 10 acres ..	38	27.2	37	34.0
1 to 5 acres ..	62	44.3	39	35.8
Under one acre ..	16	11.4	8	7.3
	140		109	

Two or three facts are clear from this. The first is that there is a greater number of large areas cultivated by one man than areas owned by one man. If we take ten acres as being, in a village chiefly if not entirely cultivated without irrigation like the present, the smaller limit of an economic holding, then we find that while only 17 per cent. of the holdings are above this limit, 23 per cent. of the areas cultivated are larger than this. There is hence a tendency for the areas of cultivation to become larger than the areas owned. The increase in not perhaps great, but we feel it represents an

* These figures will be found to be different from those on a later page, because, in this case, where a holdnig was held jointly, it has been credited to the head of the family, who may also hold other land in his own name.

increasing tendency. A second fact is that the bulk of both holdings and areas of cultivation lie between one and ten acres, an area that is too small to be economic where the cultivation is dry. Now the total area of land regularly irrigated in any way does not exceed ten acres in the village, and so the vast proportion is being not only held but cultivated in a manner which either compels the cultivators to live below what they consider to be a proper standard of life, or else to go or send some member of their families to work elsewhere during a part, or the whole, of the year. Thirdly, what has been said about those who only cultivate from one to ten acres applies with even greater force to those who cultivate less than one acre. The cultivation cannot support them, and must in these cases be considered in somewhat the same light as a labourer's allotment in England, that is to say, as a subsidiary source of income, the main source being some other occupation.

If instead of considering the total area cultivated by one man we turn to the fragmentation of such areas, we find an unexpected state of affairs. The fragmentation of the cultivation is even greater than that of the holdings. The position in the two cases is shown in the following statement :—

	Fragmentation of			
	(1) Holdings.		(2) Cultivations.	
	Number with specified number of fragments.	Per cent. of total.	Number with specified number of fragments.	Per cent. of total.
1 fragment ..	18	12.8	14	12.8
2 to 5 fragments..	75	53.6	43	39.5
6 to 10 ,, ..	34	24.3	34	31.2
11 to 15 ,, ..	8	5.7	8	7.3
16 to 20 ,, ..	4	2.9	5	4.6
21 to 25 ,, ..	1	0.7	4	3.6
Over 25 ,, ..	..	..	1	0.9

So far as the fragmentation of the land cultivated by single individuals is considered we can perhaps get an even better idea by a statement of the actual size of the plots cultivated in the village. These number 729 and their size is shown in the following table:—

*Size of plots.**	*Number of plots of each size.*
Over 20 acres	0
10 to 20 acres	8
5 to 10 acres	20
3 to 5 acres	33
2 to 3 acres	57
1 to 2 acres	148
¾ acre to 1 acre	81
½ acre to ¾ acre	149
⅜ acre to ½ acre	69
¼ acre to ⅜ acre	52
⅛ acre to ¼ acre	59
Below ⅛ acre	53

All the remarks which we have made regarding the evil effect of the minute fragmentation of holdings is of very much greater force when applied to that of cultivation. It would not be so bad if the land of the village were intensively cultivated under an irrigation system, spade cultivation being

* To get an absolutely clear idea of the situation, the following table arranged in slightly different manner may be useful:—

Size of plots.	*Number of plots of each size.*
Over 10 acres	8
9 to 10 acres	2
8 to 9 acres	1
7 to 8 acres	7
6 to 7 acres	1
5 to 6 acres	10
4 to 5 acres	18
3 to 4 acres	14
2 to 3 acres	69
1 to 2 acres	148
Below 1 acre	463

PLATE VIII.
(To face Page 52.)

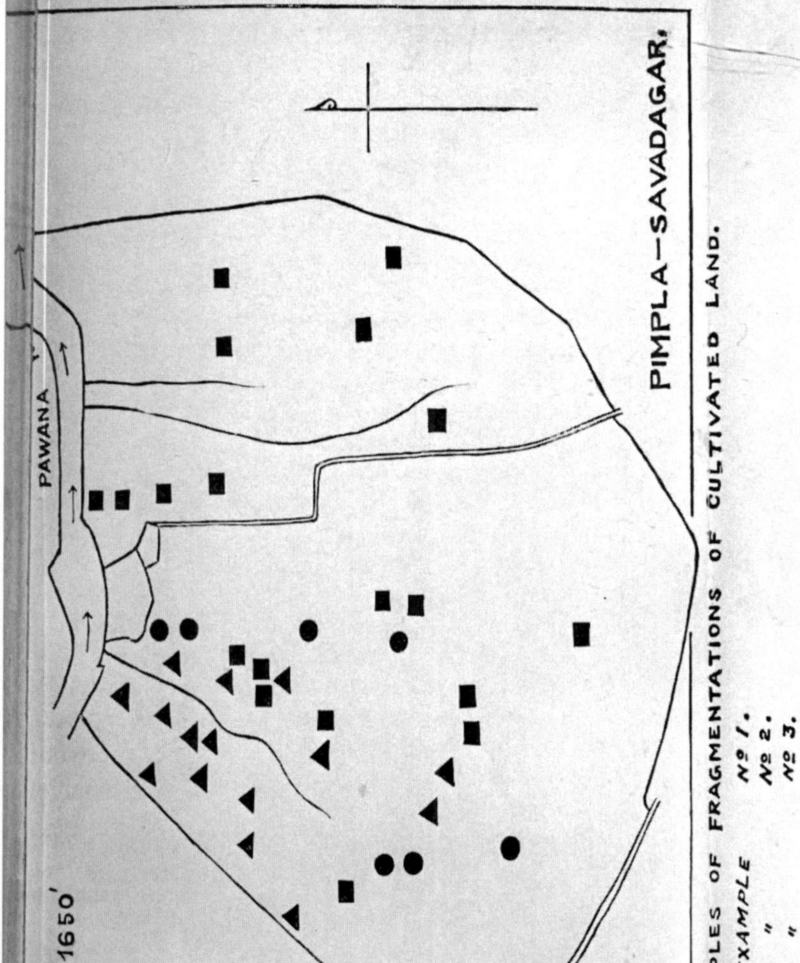

employed and high market garden conditions prevailing. This is not the case in the present village in any sense as we shall show later, and in all other circumstances it seems to be a disadvantage without any mitigating quality. If the plots are close together the evil is modified, but if these are wide apart it means endless loss of labour and time without any compensating advantage.

It would seem, however, from our many local inquiries to be the direct result of the extreme fragmentation of holdings. A man wants more land for cultivation. He can only get it by renting from a holder, and the holders who are most likely to lend are precisely those who possess only a small fragment. This is distinctly shown by the figures given above. To get large enough cultivation he has hence to take many such small patches, with the result that while the area cultivated per man is greater than the amount held per man, the number of fragments per cultivator is greater than the number of fragments per holder.

Though this conclusion, which appears directly from our figures, is one to which attention has not been called before, yet it arises directly from the excessive fragmentation of the holdings themselves. While the evil of too small uneconomic holdings might be largely removed by subletting, provided that each holding were in a few blocks only, when the holdings themselves are in small fragments, the subletting only rather intensifies the evil which it might at first sight be supposed to cure.

We are not desirous here of discussing remedies, but two results of this excessive fragmentation should, we think, have attention drawn to them.

(1) The fragmentation prevents effectually any outsider with capital from entering on cultivation on a large scale in this village. When a man may have to deal with twenty or thirty or even more landowners, in order to get a stretch of thirty or forty acres, any one of whom can spoil the continuity or self-contained character of his cultivation, nine men out

of ten will refuse to have anything to do with the scheme, unless the conditions (as in the canal irrigation tracts) are altogether exceptional.

(2) The impossibility of introducing outside cultivators with more enterprise, working on a large scale, makes the introduction of new and better ideas in agriculture more difficult. Small holders, when conditions favour the introduction of new ideas, make the most progressive cultivators in the world. They are, on the other hand, under the condition of excessive fragmentation in this village, which we believe is a typical one in the Western Deccan, about as hard to move from traditional methods as any body of men of which we can conceive.

CHAPTER IV.

VEGETATION, CROPS AND CULTIVATION OF THE VILLAGE.

WE have described the situation of the village of Pimpla Soudagar, its soils, its water available for drinking and for irrigation, and also the conditions under which the land is held and cultivated. The next matter to consider is the natural vegetation which occurs there, the crops which the people grow, and the methods which they adopt in doing so. In all this it must never be forgotten that Pimpla Soudagar is essentially a dry land village, and that the amount of irrigation is all but negligible.

A.—TREES OF THE VILLAGE.

The Deccan is not a part of India which is very highly covered with trees. Whether this has always been the case or no is a matter on which there has been very great discussion. Without entering into this controversy one may, however, say with certainty that it is not an area on which trees grow easily, at any rate so far as the part covered with the so-called black cotton soil is concerned. As soon as this soil is replaced by almost anything else, trees become far more common. As the village we are considering is right in the centre of the Deccan trap area, and hence in that covered with black cotton soil, the village is no exception to the rule. Trees are infrequent and what there are, are either near the banks of the river and of the *nalas*, or else in groups round the various wells in the village.

The total number of trees is 1,747, or slightly under two per acre. The mere number tells little, however, regarding the arboreal vegetation of the village. Out of the total number no less than 1,502, or 86 per cent., are *babul* trees (*Acacia arabica*). The *babul* is one of the few trees which seem to flourish naturally in black cotton soil. It is able, on account of its thorny character, to resist the attacks of any predatory animals, and is favoured (where the land is not wanted for other purposes) by the people as the wood of the tree is valuable for many village purposes, and as the young twigs of the tree can be used for feeding sheep and goats.

The *babul* tree, therefore, occupies a very specially favoured position for becoming common, as it seeds itself, at any rate if sheep and goats are present, and multiplies without care. We have never known *babul* trees to be planted, but there is nothing to prevent its multiplication except near the village site, where a use is found for every young tree as soon as it has become usable.

Apart from this the tree is fairly frequent on the boundaries of fields and along the courses of the *nalas*. The portions of some fields bordering on the river, especially when cut up and so rendered incapable of cultivation, are nothing but *babul* forests. One field 4½ acres in extent, contains no less than 411 trees, or nearly 100 trees per acre, but this is the only one which is anything like so thick.

Babul trees are too valuable to be allowed to attain a great size and of the total only six per cent. can be called large fully grown trees, twenty-seven per cent. are of medium size, while the remainder, or sixty-seven per cent. are only small ones. Small shrubs below three or four feet high are not included at all.

The only tree, except the *babul* which is found in a considerable number, is the mango (*Mangifera indica*). Of these trees there are 150, or 8½ per cent. of the total. The mango tree is in almost every respect absolutely the opposite of the *babul* tree. It hardly ever grows naturally, it needs considerable attention when young except under very favourable circumstances, and it is very largely, if not almost exclusively, found growing in the neighbourhood of wells, in groves, or in a few cases on the boundaries of fields and along *nalas* These trees are, of course, kept for their fruit, and they form, moreover, splendid groves under which camps can be made, and the wood is very valuable. The fruit from one good tree will usually bring about Rs. 2 to Rs. 2-8 per annum. There are *no* young mango trees in the village, and we think that none have been planted for a good many years.

Of other trees there are very few of any sort, and most of these are growing in the village site itself, either round houses or buildings,—or on the river bank close by. The following is a list of those found with the number present:—

Tree.	Marathi and English names.	Number in Village.
(1) *Fruit trees.*—		
Anona squamosa	*Sita-phal*, Custard apple	10
Zizyphus jujuba	*Bor*, Jujube tree	9
Tamarindus indica	*Chinch*, tamarind	7
Aegle marmelos	*Bael*	5
Eugenia jambolana	*Jambul*	5
Moringa pterygosperma	*Shevga*, Horse-radish tree	4
Feronia elephantum	*Kavat*, the wood apple	1
(2) *Ornamental and other trees.*—		
Ficus bengalensis	*Banyan*	8
Ficus retusa	*Nandurki*	7
Ficus glomerata	*Umber*	5
Ficus religiosa	*Pimpal*	4
Melia azidirachta	*Kadu nimb*, the neem tree	4
Plumeria acutifolia	*Pandra chapha*, the pagoda tree	3
Ailanthus excelsa	*Maharug*	2
Cordia myxa	*Bhokur*	2
Nyctanthes arbortristis	*Pari jatak*	2
Jatropha curcas	*Mogli erand*, the physic nut	2
Erythrina indica	*Pangara*	2
Hibiscus rosasinensis	*Jaswand*	2
Gossypium arboreum	*Dev-kapas*, cotton	1
Poinciana regia	*Gulmohur*, the gold mohur	1
Bombax malabaricum	*Kate*, the silk cotton tree	1
Sapindus trifoliatus	*Ritha*, the soap nut tree	1
Phoenix sylvaticus	*Shinde*, the toddy palm	7

Except for the *bor*, or jujube tree, and the *shinde* or toddy palm which are scattered about the village, chiefly on the borders of fields, these trees are almost exclusively on the village site and on the banks of the river and near the wells. Of these two, which are wild and grow on their own account probably from casually scattered seed, the former furnishes a certain amount of food for goats and sheep in its young shoots, and for man in its fruit. The second is practically no use here. Grown without irrigation and in such small numbers, it is not worth tapping for toddy, and is usually very stunted in these dry regions, and the most it can do is to furnish a few leaves for mat-making purposes.

The remainder are mostly well-known fruit and ornamental trees. The produce of all the fruit trees is eaten, but it will be noticed that in a dry village like the present that most of the commonest fruits are entirely absent. There are no guavas, no plantains, no pomegranates, no figs. This is a characteristic which every traveller in the Deccan must notice. Apart from regular fruit-growing villages with good irrigation, any kind of fruit is almost unobtainable. The fruits of most of the trees which do grow are not of much value. The custard-apple is, of course, good, but it is in season a very short time, and requires little trouble for cultivation. The tamarind and the *bael* are, of course, very useful, and the former is almost necessary in every Indian household. The fruit of a good tamarind tree is worth about Rs. 2 per annum. The *jambul* is a very pleasant fruit, but hardly an important one. The *kavat* is a very second-rate acid fruit, which however is considered worthy of sale in the bazaars.

Of the other trees, most are purely ornamental, and many, like most of the species of *Ficus*, have probably planted themselves. The *umber* tree yields fruit which are edible. The leaves of the *neem* tree are valued in medical treatment in village practice, and sometimes oil is taken from the seeds. The physic-nut, which grows round compounds, is also used as a purgative, while the soap-nut is generally used for washing clothes. The tree-cotton, grown near the temple, furnishes material for making sacred threads.

On the whole, therefore, this village illustrates the treeless character of the Deccan, except as regards *babul* and in a minor degree such trees as jujube and toddy palm. For the rest, with the exception of mango topes near the wells (all composed of old trees) and a few ornamental trees and others useful in various directions near the houses, there is extremely little tree growth.

B.—Herbaceous Vegetation.

The natural herbaceous vegetation is best illustrated by the weed herbage found in and between the fields. As so much of the land is under cultivation in the rainy season, and moreover few weeds ripen then, the plants found throughout were collected in December, January, and February. At this time of year almost the whole of the weeds are in a form which can be easily identified.*

A complete list of the wild plants found is given in the Appendix. This list is important, as we think it is typical of much of the medium black soil area of the Deccan, where there is no irrigation. The plants have been classified in the order of their frequency, with the following result :—

Plants noted as *very common*	23
Plants noted as *common*	17
Plants noted as *fairly common*	13
Plants *frequently found, but not common* ..	18
Plants noted as *not common*	45
Plants escaped from cultivation	10
Total	126

* We are very much indebted to Mr. R. K. Bhide, Assistant Economic Botanist to the Government of Bombay, for both collecting and identifying the village weeds for us.

Most of these plants have little or no economic interest, but a few of them are serious weeds of cultivation, and so are exceedingly important. Among these are six which are considered by the people as the worst. These are :—

1.	*Hariali*	.. *Cynodon dactylon.*
2.	*Kunda*	.. *Ischæmum pilosum.*
3.	*Lowala* or *Nagarmotha*	.. *Cyperus rotundus.*
4.	*Godhadi*	.. *Heylandia latebrosa.*
5.	*Barbada*	.. *Indigofera glandulosa.*
6.	*Vàsanvel*	.. *Cocculus villosa.*

Of these it will be seen two (1 and 2) are true grasses, one (3) is a sedge, the next two (4 and 5) are leguminous plants, while the last belongs to the natural order *Menispermaceæ.*

With regard to each of these, considered as weeds, we may remark as follows :—

(1) *Hariali* is one of the worst weeds in the tropics throughout the world, though the grass produced makes an excellent fodder. It invades cultivated land everywhere, however, and becomes an exceeding nuisance. In the United States it has been called "an aggressive and pestiferous" weed, and it can hardly be worse anywhere than it is in the Deccan. The village under discussion is not so seriously affected as many we have seen, and there are no actual patches which the cultivators have ceased to plough owing to infestation with this and the next-named weed (*kunda*). But there are hardly any fields without it. The people recognise it can be got rid of by hand-digging and removing in the dry season, or by repeated ploughing with a turnover plough. It rapidly spreads from the field boundaries if allowed to grow there. But the life of a Deccan cultivator is one long battle with *hariali* and *kunda.*

(2) *Kunda* shares with *hariali* the hatred of the cultivators, as it is perhaps even worse than the latter when it gets hold of a piece of land. *Hariali* grass is of some use

as fodder. *Kunda* is practically of no value for this purpose. It has to be got rid of by precisely the same methods as *hariali*, but one good ploughing in the cold weather with a turnover plough is said completely to eradicate it. Both these grasses are very common in the village.

(3) *Lowala* or *Nagarmotha*, where it occurs, is a sedge perhaps worse and more hard to get rid of than the two foregoing grasses. It is, however, more limited to low-lying and moist places, but there it is a very great nuisance. It has not only very resistant rootstocks, but these are furnished with hard tubers from which new plants will arise, and which easily separate from the rootstocks when the latter are pulled out. These tubers have their economic use and are frequently collected in villages for preparing scented powders for use on festive occasions, as *masala* for anointing the bodies of both men and women. The method adopted for getting rid of this weed is the same as that described for *hariali*. Constant harrowing will also remove it to a great extent, but must be done at regular intervals as soon as the *lowala* shows above ground.

(4) *Godhadi* (a term which means, "spreading like a quilt"), is recognised as a very bad weed, and it is as common as *hariali*. It flowers from February to June and can be uprooted easily. But at the time of the year at which it flowers and seeds little cultivation is going on, and as a result it remains very common, damaging every crop among which it grows. Its only redeeming feature is that cattle will eat the herbage, and hence it is to a small extent collected for their benefit.

(5) *Barbada*, a form of wild indigo, is one of the commonest annual weeds. It flowers from August to December, and could probably be easily kept in hand by frequent and regular interculture of the crops. As it is, it is looked upon as an unmitigated nuisance. It is eaten by cattle when young, but when older it is of no use whatever.

(6) *Vasanvel* is one of the worst weeds, and its deep roots are very difficult to remove. The roots are in fact often

four or five feet deep. If any parts are left in the soil, the weed will spring up again and will destroy the crop by twining round the plants and smothering them. It flowers in December.

These are the most fatal weeds, but there are many others which regularly do a great deal of damage. In fact, the destruction of weeds must form a very distinct item in any programme for the economic development of a Deccan village like Pimpla Soudagar.

A few though not many of the wild plants of the village serve some economic purpose, though its importance can hardly be valued in money. Apart from the grasses, most of which give some herbage, and some like *marvel* (*Andropogon annulatus*) are very valuable fodder grasses, the following notes on their uses may be of value :—

1. At certain stages of their growth the following plants are eaten with avidity by cattle or buffaloes, and hence may be classed as minor fodder plants.

a. *Heylandia latebrosa* (Leguminosæ).—This, as already noted, is collected for fodder.

b. *Indigofera glandulosa* (Leguminosæ).—This is eaten by cattle when young only.

c. *Psoralia corylifolia* (Leguminosæ), known as *bavachi*, is found in moist places and is liked by cattle, but is not collected.

d. *Desmodium diffusum* (Leguminosæ), known as *chikta* is greedily eaten by cattle, but, unfortunately, it is not very common.

e. *Indigofera cordifolia* (Leguminosæ).—Buffaloes eat this plant readily when young.

f. *Crotolaria linifolia* (Leguminosæ).—A fairly uncommon plant, but eaten by cattle when found.

g. *Cyanotis axillaris* (Commelinaceæ).—This is a fairly common plant, eaten, when young, by cattle.

h. *Marsdenia volubilis* (Asclepiadaceæ)—Cattle are said to eat the leaves of this plant.

This is obviously not a complete list of the plants which along with most of the grasses form fodder for cattle. It gives, however, the most important of them.

2. One plant, *Pennisetum alopecurus* or *mohl,* is a grass which is recognised to have excellent binding characters with soils. It occurs generally along streams, and is sometimes planted on the corners and sides of borders of fields, or embankments. Soil on which it is planted resists erosion by water. It cannot be eradicated without deep digging if once it is established.

3. Two or three plants are regularly used for medicinal purposes. Others may be collected, but their use is not so generally known among the people.

a. *Eclipta erecta* or *maka* (Compositæ).—This common plant occurs chiefly round dwellings, manure pits, or other places where refuse is thrown. It is recognised as valuable in venereal diseases.

b *Tribulus terrestris* or *sara a* (Zygophylaceæ) grows chiefly on light or *mal* lands. Its fruits are used medicinally.

c. *Solanum xanthocarpum* or *bhui ringni* (Solanaceæ) has roots occasionally used in medicine.

4. Two or three plants are used for fibre, but only rarely, for ropes are provided by the village *mangs* and these are almost always prepared here from agave plants. However, the wild plants of the genus *Hibiscus* and of the genus *Corchorus* are occasionally used.

5. A number of the wild plants found are obviously escapes from cultivation, and of course their produce, whatever be its nature, is used when found. Such escapes which occur wild are (*a*) the *brinjal* or egg plant (very common); (*b*) *Brassica juncea* or *rai-mohori,* a mustard; (*c*) *Hibiscus cannabinus,* the well-known fibre plant known as *ambadi* or Deccan hemp; (*d*) linseed; (*e*) *tur* or pigeon pea, the well-known

pulse; (*f*) field peas; (*g*) *udid* or *mung* (*Phaseolus mungo*); (*h*) *Pencedanum granolum* or *balantshep*; (*i*) *Foeniculum vulgare* or *badishep*; (*j*) the carrot, and (*k*) *til* or sesamum.

C.—Implements for Cultivation.

In a village like that which we are considering, which lies in a large measure apart from the more progressive parts of the country, owing to its being carried on almost entirely by dry cultivation, the implements in use for producing crops are of the primitive kind which were universal a few years ago, and which are only now slowly and gradually being replaced by more efficient, and, we may add, more expensive ones. The implements in use at present (1915) are shown in the following list with their costs:—

	Rs.	a.	p.		Rs.	a.	p.
(1) Plough, complete with yokes ..	15	0	0	to	18	0	0
(2) Harrow, complete with yoke ..	3	0	0				
(3) Light harrow for covering the seed, called *pharat*	3	0	0				
(4) Seed drill, complete	6	0	0				
(5) Heavy seed drill (*moghan*) ..	7	0	0				
(6) Bullock hoe	3	0	0				
(7) Spade or *kudal*	0	8	0				
(8) Pick-axe	0	8	0				
(9) Hand harrow (*khurpa*)	0	4	0				
(10) Sickle	0	12	0				
(11) Cart	75	0	0	to	90	0	0

Thus to get a complete set of implements as required by a good cultivator (except for the cart) will cost from Rs. 39 to Rs. 42. All can be made in the village, and two carpenters (see above) are maintained for the purpose of making and repairing them. These are paid in kind and not in cash, and for all repairs to village implements they each get (as

PLATE IX.
(To face Page 64.)

Agricultural Implements, with village *Chavdi* or "Town Hall" in the background.
Plough. Bullock-hoe, Harrow. Seed-drill. Light Harrow (for covering seed).

baluta) one *palla* (280 pounds) of grain and five hundred sheaves of *jowari* or *bajri* with the heads of corn on them. Beyond this they are paid in cash for new implements required, and for any other extra work which they do. The bigger cultivators are first attended to, and generally pay extra for the concession.

This is the system which has been universal in Deccan villages, and is maintained still in almost all places, at least at those which are off the main roads.

Practically all the implements are made of *babul* wood, and are of the patterns ordinarily in use for soil of this class,* there is hence no need to describe them. A few notes may be made, however, about certain among them.

(1) The heavy seed drill is a somewhat peculiar implement. It is exactly like the ordinary drill, only having a body double the size in order to sow the seed very deeply during the *rabi* season. At this season (September and October) it is essential to put in seed very deep, say, four to six inches, into the parts of the soil which still hold plenty of moisture. Hence the heavy seed drill, which is worked by two, and even occasionally by three pairs of bullocks.

(2) The ordinary harrow in use here is only two and a half feet wide, but the block of which the body is made is short, thick and heavy, when compared with the light harrow or *pharat*. It is chiefly used to prepare the land following the plough.

(3) The light harrow or *pharat* is wider than the last, being usually three and a half feet broad. This is generally used to cover the seed, following the seed drill.

The draught required for each of the implements used with bullocks is shown below:—

(1) Plough—from one to four pairs of bullocks, according to season and class of work.

(2) Harrow—usually one to two pairs of bullocks.

* Cf. Kelkar—"Indigenous Implements of the Bombay Presidency," Bulletin No. 66, Bombay Department of Agriculture (1915).

(3) Light harrow (*pharat*)—one pair of bullocks.

(4) Seed drill—usually one pair of bullocks for sowing in the *kharif* season, and up to three pairs of bullocks for sowing the *rabi* crops.

A man fitted out with such a complete set of implements and land sufficient to put them to full use would require also four pairs of bullocks in his stable. He would, however, only need these for about one hundred days in the year at the most, and as already stated, they would be available for the remainder of the year for other purposes. It is this fact which has led to the development of carting on the roads as a secondary occupation by many of the people of this and similar villages.

We have already referred to the fact that the use of the modern iron plough has made little progress in this as in most dry land villages. Only two cultivators in 1915 hired such ploughs for trial for a few days. The general opinion formed and expressed with regard to them is that they are efficient on land in fairly dry condition, and are well worth having under such conditions as they do better work with less expenditure of bullock power. When the land is wet and sticky, the people consider that there is no advantage, and that the country wooden plough answers as well, or better.

At present the whole number of the larger farm implements held in the village with 1,006 acres of cultivation and a population of 556 is as follows :—

Ploughs	25
Harrows	35
Light harrows ..	30
Seed drills	30
Carts	20

D.—Crops of the Village.

The actual cropping of the village at a number of dates n the past thirty years is as follows. The figures have been extracted from the official records, kept in the first instance by the village *kulkarni* or accountant, and show to what extent the character of the cultivation has varied. The total area of the village has remained constant at 1,065 acres, and the land unassessed and recognised to be uncultivable has been throughout 59-60 acres.

	1885—1886	1891—1892	1894—1895	1900—1901	1905—1906	1913—1914	1914—1915	1915—1916
	ac.	ac.	ac.	ac.	ac.	ac.	ac.	ac.
Nett area under crop	910	803	807	759	864	874	915	726
Fallow, *i.e.*, cultivable area not under crop	96	203	199	247	142	131	91	280
Area double cropped.	109	32	100	241	3	3	16	25
Grain Crops.								
Jowar (kharif) / Jowar (rabi) ..	268	218	169	288	291	151 / 490	162 / 341	131 / 215
Bajri	191	250	273	273	183	129	49	75
Rice	..	..	..	..	..	..	..	6
Wheat	261	218	162	110	275	39	120	55
Pulse Crops.								
Tur	26	14	17	23	11	13	6	4
Gram	149	29	128	212	10	3	74	31
Peas	26	25	9	23	13	4	27	41
Other pulses.. ..	5	7	..	30	11	4	2	23
Vegetables, Roots, &c...	36	49	100	29	54	13	116	84
Spices (chiefly chillies)	8	under 1	9	2	7	under 1	..	under 1
Other Crops.								
Niger seed	46	22	18	8	..	21	12	68
Groundnut	1	3	13	2	5	7	10	9
Sugar-cane	..	..	6	..	3	..	..	7
Sann and ambadi * (for fibre).. ..	1	..	2	2	4	1	1	1

We will deal with each of the more important of these crops separately as they are managed and cultivated in the village, but before doing so let us consider certain facts disclosed by the above figures.

The fallow area represents in a village like this the whole of the cultivable area which is not under crop. It includes the

* Sann=*Crotolaria uncea*; Ambadi=*Hibiscus cannabinus.*

land intentionally left fallow, the area left for grazing, the area (always large in villages on the black soil, with the ordinary implements used in Deccan villages) which cannot be sown because the proper time for sowing is lost owing to pressure of work, and the area which, owing to the vagaries of the rain, was never in proper condition for sowing. The chief causes of the very large alternations in the figures are the variations in the area included under the third and fourth of these headings. If the sowing season is long, then almost all the land may be sown : if the rain is not such as to give many opportunities of sowing, the fallow area may be large. The minimum as represented by 1885-86 and 1914-15 may be not much more than ninety acres or about 9 per cent. of the cultivable area : the maximum may reach 280 acres (1915-16), or 27·8 per cent. The extremes are shown in the two successive years 1914-15 and 1915-16, and probably are connected with the admirable sowing conditions which prevailed in the *kharif* sowing season in 1914, and the very difficult ones which occurred at the same time of year in 1915.*

But the minimum area of uncultivated land is large, and this is perhaps more the result of the poverty of some of the soil, and of the need at least for some grazing area in excess of what is provided by the unassessed and uncultivable lands. At first sight this large area of fallow seems to represent a very low stage of agricultural progress, and we think it really does so. In a more developed condition the implements would be such as to permit the rapid sowing of the land even in a bad season, and the growth of fodder crops would make unnecessary the leaving of much land for grazing. But, in spite of this, it must never be forgotten that there is a very considerable area of very poor land, which barely pays to put under crop at any time, and which a good cultivator abandons to his cattle at any time without much regret. The really inferior soil, according to the revenue survey, amounts to no less than 235 acres, or 23 per cent. of the total area.

*For monthly rainfall in these two years see table on page 3

The area which is double-cropped is a measure of the intensity of the cultivation in the village. It varies extremely owing to the very large variations in the character of the rainfall, and to the necessities of the people. It reached its highest point in 1900-01, in the year following one of the very serious famine years in the Deccan. In this village it very largely, as we shall see, consists of land growing peas and *rabi jowar*, in succession, the former for the Poona market.

The actual crops grown in the village have not varied very much, and the list is almost the same as it was thirty years ago. Rice and sugar-cane have appeared but the area devoted to them is exceedingly small. On the other hand, the proportionate area given to different crops and to different classes of crops has varied very much, and we will consider each class, and, in some measure, the causes to which the variation is due.

The area under grain has been on the whole fairly constant, except for the last year under record. The actual figures being, for the years given below, as follows :—

1885-86	..	..	720 acres.
1891-92	..	..	686 ,,
1894-95	..	..	604 ,,
1900-01	..	..	671 ,,
1905-06	..	..	749 ,,
1913-14	..	..	809 ,,
1914-15	..	..	672 ,,
1915-16	..	..	482 ,,

This area consists, however, of crops occupying two very different economic functions. All the crops, except wheat, are essentially grown for home consumption. Wheat, on the other hand, is a cash crop, hardly used (except for the inferior straw as fodder) at home, and usually sold for an immediate money return. We will discuss the reasons for the decline of wheat later (see pages 93-96), but the following table shows the percentage of the grain area occupied by the two classes of cereals :—

	Per cent. of grain area occupied by all cereals except wheat.	Per cent. of grain area occupied by wheat.
	%	%
1885-86	63.8	36.2
1891-92	68.2	31.8
1894-95	73.2	26.8
1900-01	83.6	16.4
1905-06	63.3	36.7
1913-14	95.2	4.8
1914-15	82.1	17.9
1915-16	88.6	11.4

The proportion of the grain area occupied by wheat, that is by cash-crop cereals, has very much declined. This, however, as we shall see is not due to the devotion of a less area of land to cash crops, but to the discovery that fresh vegetables for the Poona market, groundnuts, and other crops pay a working cultivator better than wheat.

The relative area occupied by *bajri* and *jowar* is a very interesting study. The former is exclusively a *kharif* crop: the latter may be either a *kharif* or a *rabi* crop. The former is grown on light land: the latter on both light and heavy land. The former gives plenty of fodder of an inferior kind: the latter gives the best fodder in the market. The percentages of each of these on the area under grain crops, omitting wheat, is given in the following table at different periods :—

<table>
<tr><th></th><th>Percentage of area occupied by kharif jowar.</th><th>Percentage of area occupied by rabi jowar.</th><th>Percentage of area occupied by bajri.</th></tr>
<tr><td></td><td>%</td><td>%</td><td>%</td></tr>
<tr><td>1885-86</td><td colspan="2">58.4</td><td>41.6</td></tr>
<tr><td>1891-92</td><td colspan="2">46.6</td><td>53.4</td></tr>
<tr><td>1894-95</td><td colspan="2">38.2</td><td>61.8</td></tr>
<tr><td>1900-01</td><td colspan="2">51.3</td><td>48.7</td></tr>
<tr><td>1905-06</td><td colspan="2">61.4</td><td>38.6</td></tr>
<tr><td>1913-14</td><td>19.6</td><td>63.6</td><td>16.8</td></tr>
<tr><td>1914-15</td><td>29.3</td><td>61.9</td><td>8.8</td></tr>
<tr><td>1915-16</td><td>31.1</td><td>51.1</td><td>17.8</td></tr>
</table>

These figures show a very large decrease in the proportion of *bajri* cultivated in the village, and, we believe, a very considerable increase in the amount of *kharif jowar*. The increase in *rabi jowar* largely replaces wheat: that of *kharif* jowar replaces *bajri*. We believe this is due to the increased value of fodder in recent years, and to the existence of types of *jowar* which will grow well on the lighter lands formerly almost entirely given up to *bajri*. The reduction in the proportionate area of *bajri* is reflected in the figures for the sub-division (taluka) in which the village is situated. There the proportion of the *jowar* to the total combined area of *jowar* and *bajri* has been progressively increasing. Thus in the years between 1885-86 and 1889-90 the *jowar* formed 42.4% of the combined acreage, while in 1908-09 to 1912-13 it formed no less than 47.9 per cent. Thus the relative importance of *jowar* is increasing in the whole neighbourhood as well as in the village under study, though not to such a very marked extent.

It is difficult to make any general discussion of the pulse crops as a whole, as they serve (in this village) three different purposes. The *tur* (*Cajanus indicus*) is a pulse generally sown in rows with the *bajri* or, to a less extent, with the *jowar*, which form the staple cultivations of the village. It forms essentially a complement to the *bajri* crop, while at the same time being the chief pulse eaten in the village. The gram, on the other hand, is a complement to the wheat cultivation, and will, on the whole, be found to rise and fall in area, in close correspondence with the wheat. The peas, again, are a market crop, chiefly being reaped in the green condition for sale as a vegetable. As these serve such different purposes no general conclusions as to this class of crops are possible.

The small residue of other pulse crops consists of *kulthi* (*Dolichos biflorus*), *udid* (*Phaseolus radiatus*), and *mug* (*Phaseolus mungo*), *chavli* (*Vigna catiang*), and *val* (*Dolichos lablab*). All are grown for the grain, but none to anything more than a very minor extent. *Val* never has been cultivated over more than one acre. The others in 1915-16 occupied land as follows :—

Kulthi	2 acres.
Udid	12 acres.
Mug	7 acres.
Chavli	2 acres.

The crops classed as vegetables occupy a rather large area in the village, and their cultivation is very characteristic here, especially that of carrots. The actual crops in three of the years discussed for which alone we have full data were as follows :—

	1885-86.	1891-92.	1915-16.
	Ac.	Ac.	Ac.
Carrots	32	38	78
Methi (fenugreek) .. .. }	4	1	1
Bhendi (Ladies' fingers) .. }		4	5
Onions..	—	6	—

The vegetable crops are essentially, and to an increasing extent, carrots. Onions appear occasionally, while minor vegetable crops, like fenugreek and *bhendi*, form a constant though small element of the cultivation. The importance of carrots depends on the presence of the Poona market, and we will describe their cultivation in detail later.

The remaining crops do not seem to call for any general remarks, and will be discussed better, so far as concerns niger seed, groundnut and sugarcane, under their separate headings. *Sann* and *ambadi* (or Deccan hemp) are simply grown for fibre as a scattering among other crops, and do not need special mention.

E.—Rotations of the Village.

Before dealing with the separate crops there are two matters which should be considered, namely, the rotations in which they are grown and the nature of the seed supply from which they are produced. With regard to the rotations, we do not think that there appears any clear rational arrangement in their succession, but we give them for what they are worth.

In the first place we have those crops which are frequently grown continuously for five years on the same land. The only ones in this position are *bajri* and *jowar*. In the latter case the matter can be varied by growing different varieties (*shalu nilwa, argadi*, etc.) though there is no regularity about the way in which they replace one another.

A second arrangement was that of growing these same crops for four years continuously and then making a change. This is usually then followed by carrots or wheat, or a fallow in the fifth year.

Still a third system is to have crops three years continuously on the same land and then make a change. Those which are so cultivated are *jowari*, *bajri* and wheat. The last crop is grown continuously for three years, but only very arely.

Finally, far more common than any of these is the large number of cases in which the same crop is grown for two years. Even here such continuous cropping for two years with the same crop is limited to *bajri*, *jowari* and wheat, the last named being rarely so treated.

Taking the actual plants on the ground in 1915 and the records for the previous year, it would seem that the following successions of crops are used, and are common in the proportion indicated :—

(1) *Jowar* followed by *bajri* .. .. 15% of area.
(2) *Bajri* followed by *jowar* .. .. 15% of area.
(3) *Jowar* followed by *jowar* .. .. 10% of area.
(4) *Jowar* followed by carrots .. .. 9% of area.
(5) Carrots followed by *jowar* .. .. 9% of area.
(6) *Bajri* followed by *bajri* .. .. 8% of area.
(7) Carrots followed by *bajri* .. .. 8% of area.
(8) *Jowar* followed by niger seed .. .. 8% of area.
(9) *Bajri* followed by fallow .. .. 5% of area.
(10) *Jowar* followed by fallow .. .. 2% of area.
(11) Wheat followed by *jowar* .. .. 2% of area.
(12) *Jowar* followed by wheat .. .. 2% of area.
(13) *Bajri* followed by carrots .. .. 1% of area.
(14) *Bajri* followed by wheat .. .. 1% of area.
(15) Carrots followed by wheat .. .. 1% of area.
(16) Peas followed by *jowar* .. .. 1% of area.
(17) *Jowar* followed by groundnut .. .. ½% of area.
(18) Groundnut followed by *jowar* .. .. ½% of area.
(19) *Bajri* followed by groundnut .. .. ½% of area.
(20) Groundnut followed by *bajri* .. .. ½% of area.
(21) Carrots followed by gram .. .. ½% of area.
(22) Wheat followed by gram .. .. ½% of area.

The relative popularity of these successions may be indicated by the frequency with which they occurred in the two years which were carefully studied. If the most frequent among them (*jowari-bajri*) be taken as 100, then the frequency of the other successions is indicated by the followed figures :—

Bajri and *jowar*	98
Jowar and *jowar*	60
Bajri and fallow	50
Bajri and *bajri*	42
Carrots and *bajri*	42
Carrots and *jowar*	36
Wheat and *jowar* *Jowar* and wheat	32
Jowar and niger seed	20
Jowar and fallow	20
Jowar and carrots	18
Bajri and groundnut; groundnut and *bajri*	18
Peas and *jowar*	16
Bajri and wheat	15
Wheat and gram	12
Groundnut and *jowar*	12
Bajri and carrots	8
Carrots and wheat	8
Jowar and groundnut	6
Carrots and gram	6

Thus, taken crop by crop, we have—

(1) *Jowar* is followed by crops in this order of frequency: (a) *Bajri*, (b) *Jowar*, (c) Wheat, (d) Niger, (e) Fallow, (f) Carrots, (g) Groundnut.

(2) *Bajri* is followed by crops in this order of frequency: (a) *Jowar*, (b) Fallow, (c) *Bajri*, (d) Groundnut, (e) Wheat, (f) Carrots.

(3) Carrots (usually with peas), which is the third crop in area, is followed by other crops in this order of frequency: (a) *Bajri*, (b) *Jowar*, (c) Wheat, (d) Gram.

(4) Wheat, (which stands next in area) is followed by other crops in the order given, (a) *Jowar*, (b) Gram.

(5) Groundnut is generally followed by *bajri* or *jowar*, the latter a little less frequently.

(6) Peas are usually followed by *jowar*.

There does not seem very much obvious reason for these successions of crops. The perpetuation of fallows is perhaps one of the most striking features of them, and this fact (as already remarked) shows how really little advanced the agriculture is. This, of course, most frequently follows *bajri* on the lighter land of the village.

This question of the use of fallows under the present conditions is a very interesting one. The alternative to a fallow is usually either manuring or alternation with a leguminous crop. Of these, the former is in a large measure inadmissible as we shall show below, as the uncertainty of the suitability and timely character of the rainfall makes expensive manuring on dry land a very risky matter. It is far more risky indeed than anyone who has had only to do with agriculture in Europe can conceive, and when it involves an out-of-pocket expenditure, as for the purchase of artificial manures, is a perfect gamble. On the other hand, the alternation with leguminous crops has not gone very far, largely, we believe, because of the little value which most leguminous crops, except perhaps gram, have when they are grown under our conditions. *Udid* and most of the other pulses yield very little profit per acre. Groundnut, on the other hand, is very profitable, but until the introduction of the newer varieties which grow quickly it could not be grown without at least having irrigation in reserve. The newer varieties—Spanish peanut and Japan groundunt,—which ripen in from three to five months, have however altered the situation, and it is quite possible that their use will become more general on the lighter lands where fallows have been most necessary and common. The rotations of groundnut with *bajri* and *jowar* form two per cent. of the rotations cultivated in the village, and there seems perhaps some prospect of this area increasing.

We will, however, return to this point in discussing the groundnut crop.

A few years ago the favourite rotation in the village was, according to the evidence of the people, wheat and gram. This has been very largely abandoned, according to the people, because the rain has become more uncertain and because of the increasing need of fodder. Wheat gives a very poor fodder and gram gives almost none. Thus to avoid these two troubles they have taken much more largely to *jowar* and *bajri* both of which give much fodder as well as grain.

At the time of our inquiries one of the favourite rotations was carrots and peas grown together, rotated with *jowar* and *bajri*. This is manifestly a special practice depending on the demand for carrots in the Poona market.

The character of the rotation is determined, we were informed, too by the want of labour,—for a very large number of people go away to work in Kirkee or Poona. The extent to which this is the case will be dealt with in a succeeding chapter, but it affects the rotations used, by determining that the crops grown shall be those which do not need the labour all at one time even though the yield is a little smaller. This is one of the reasons which leads to the present popularity of carrots and peas as a rotation with *jowar* and *bajri*, or these grain crops with each other.

In the absence of rotations, which are recognised to have special advantages, the people have developed the system of mixed crops to a very great extent, and their preference for this form of cultivation has rapidly increased in recent years so far as we can judge from the crop records in the village. If we take the years 1913 and 1915 we find that the mixtures which are commonly used are as follows, in order of frequency :—

(1) Carrots with peas.
(2) *Bajri*, *tur*, with *kulthi*.
(3) *Bajri*, *tur*, *kulthi*, *ambadi*.
(4) *Bajri*, *tur*.

(5) *Bajri, kulthi.*
(6) *Bajri,* niger.
(7) *Bajri, kulthi, ambadi.*
(8) *Argadi,-jowar,* and *kulthi.*
(9) Wheat, with peas.
(10) *Argadi-jowar,* niger.
(11) Carrots and peas, with *ambadi*
(12) *Nilwa-jowar* and *tur.*
(13) *Bajri, tur, udid, ambadi.*
(14) *Bajri, udid, mug.*
(15) *Shalu-jowar* and *bhendi.*

It will be seen from this that in essence these mixtures are—

(1) A grain crop like *bajri* or *jowari* mixed with a leguminous crop like *tur*, or in the case of a *rabi* grain crop like wheat with peas,—the latter only very occasionally.

(2) Carrots with peas.

We have, mixed with these, a small amount of *ambadi* and one or two other crops, while on light land niger is fairly frequently mixed with *bajri* instead of *tur.*

In the case of *tur,* the seeds are sown in lines with the main crop, there being three lines of the main crop and one line of the admixture. With niger and *ambadi* the same system is adopted frequently, but usually with those as with other mixtures the seed is mixed with that of the main crop before sowing, or else is separately broadcasted over the field after the drilling of the main crop is finished.

Such being the succession of crops and the mixtures of crops in general use, we must now discuss each of the important ones among these with reference to the methods adopted for its cultivation and the part which it takes in the life of the village.

F.—Jowar. (Sorghum Vulgare.)

As in practically all the drier parts of Western India, at any rate where the soil is moderately good, *jowar* occupies the first place among crops in the life of the village. It fills the largest area of all the grain crops, and it forms the staple food both of the men and the animals. As has already been noted, a few years ago a good deal of the land now devoted to *jowar* was devoted to wheat. The causes given for the abandonment of wheat in favour of *jowar* have already been indicated in part. These are (1) the increasing uncertainty of the rains, and (2) the need for fodder as well as grain. Beyond this the people also state that the cost of the seed in the case of wheat is very high, and that this is an out-of-pocket charge. A high out-of-pocket cost is almost always fatal to a dry land crop in Western India. Finally, it is usually also stated that the labour required to cultivate a large area of *jowar* is much less than that needed for wheat. In one case in 1915 one man was cultivating without help from fifteen to twenty acres of *jowar* in one block. This is not considered possible in the case of other crops and particularly in the case of wheat.

The land occupied by *jowar* is the best in the village, and this crop is hence largely concentrated on the flatter, deeper lands on the east and south of the village. In this area the soils, light black to medium black in character, are richer, heavier, and more retentive of moisture than in other parts of the area. On the extreme south, however, shallower and poorer lands prevail and naturally *jowar* gives place to some extent to *bajri*: the same is the case on the west of the village.

As is well known, *jowar* is grown both in the *kharif* and in the *rabi* season, the latter being considerably most common. The areas devoted to the two crops were, in 1915-16, 215 acres of *rabi jowar* and 131 acres of *kharif jowar*. The land necessary for *rabi jowar* is better than for the *kharif* crop, as the crop in the *rabi* season has largely to depend on the water stored in the soil during the previous rainy season.

The preliminary cultivation in the case of *kharif* (*nilwa* or *argadi*) *jowar* is very small indeed. The land is, in fact, simply harrowed two to four times before sowing, after sufficient rain has fallen in June, and then the seed is sown with the drill. The seed per acre is only six to eight pounds, either alone or mixed with pulse, generally *tur* or *kulthi*, at the rate of two pounds per acre. The seed germinates within ten days if the moisture in the soil is sufficient. After this the only attention the crop gets is one interculturing with the bullock hoe a month after sowing, and watching to scare birds when the grain is forming.

The quality of the seed used by the people in the *kharif* season was examined by our friend, the late Mr. G. D. Mehta. He collected samples of seed of all kinds actually being sown, from a large number of cultivators, and the results which we present are, throughout, his work. He found that the quality of the *jowar* seed was very variable, both as to purity and power of germination. The examination of thirty-six samples of *jowar* seed actually being sown in the *kharif* season gave the following results :—

(1) *Purity of seed.*
Highest quality seed ..100 per cent. purity.
Lowest quality seed .. 92 per cent. purity.
Average purity of seed .. 98.2 per cent.

(2) *Germinating power of seed.*
Highest quality seed .. 94 per cent. germination.
Lowest quality seed .. 59 per cent. germination.
Average germination of seed .. .. .. 84.6 per cent.

(3) *Proportion of useful seed.*
Highest quality seed .. 93.2 per cent. good
Lowest quality seed .. 54.2 per cent. good
Average sample contained.. 83.1 per cent. good seed.

So far as purity was concerned, the impurity was chiefly

dirt, and the only weed seeds mixed with the *jowar* were *Alysicarpus rugosus* (*shewra*) and *Indigofera glandulosa* (*barbada*), both common annual weeds in the village. Over 40 per cent. of the samples contained the seeds of one or both of these weeds, the former being the more frequent.

The germination was very bad, and varied enormously. The best seed was as good as is ever found in the Deccan, the worst was worse than we have ever seen. The proportion of samples of various grades is shown in the following table :—

Useful seed.	Proportion of samples with this percentage.
	%
90 to 100%	22
80 to 90%	50
70 to 80%	22
60 to 70%	3
50 to 60%	3

The very bad samples were thus not very numerous, but the proportion of moderately bad ones was quite large. No less than twenty-eight per cent. of the samples give less than 80% of useful seed.

The crop is ready for harvesting by October or November when it is cut with the sickle, is spread in the fields for a week to dry in the sun, and is then tied in bundles and carried to the threshing yard. The ears are separated from the stalk by hand, and the threshing done under the bullocks' feet. The grain is winnowed in the wind after the usual manner, and the grain is then ready for use.

In the case of *rabi* (*shalu*) *jowar* the land is ploughed at a convenient time in the rains and gets at least three harrowings at an interval of a fortnight. The first harrowing is done with two pairs of bullocks, and the later ones with one pair. The seed is sown in September or October (*Ashwin*) at the rate of about eight pounds per acre. A four-coultered heavy seed drill is used, with two pairs of bullocks, and the seed is planted six inches deep. The seed is covered by the light harrow termed *pharat.* The seed is usually from a cultivator's own stock, but if it has to be borrowed or bought the price is high, generally six to eight seers* per rupee.

The seed used in the sowing of *rabi jowar* in the case concerned was of somewhat better quality than in the *kharif* season except for the fact that out of twenty-seven samples, three were so badly attacked with weevils that they were excluded from the following average figures. Of the other twenty-four, the average purity was 97.8 per cent., the average germination was 90.8 per cent., while the mean proportion of useful seed was 88.8 per cent.

Only one sample contained weed seed,—in this case a species of *Amaranthus.* The variation was considerable, as the following table including the weevilled samples shows:—

Useful seed.		Proportion of Samples with this Percentage.
		%
90 to 100%	..	25
80 to 90%	..	26
70 to 80%	..	4
40 to 50%	..	4
10 to 20%	..	11

Thus nineteen per cent. of the samples gave less than 80% of useful seed.

No interculture is given with *rabi jowar*, and after planting it merely requires watching when the crop is maturing, in order to keep off birds. These are particularly destructive at the time of the *rabi* harvest, and in this village it was no uncommon sight to see ears without any grains in them whatever due to their devastations. The crop is harvested about the middle of February, as it ripens in about four and a half months.

*One seer = two pounds,

With *rabi jowar*, harvesting is done with the sickle as with the *kharif* crop, or much more frequently by uprooting the whole plants. The cut crop remains in the field for a week in order to dry, and is then tied in bundles and taken to the threshing yard.

The *rabi* crop is said to suffer when the rainfall is particularly heavy, largely owing to washing of soil which takes place on the uneven land, and also largely to the enormous cracking of the soil which takes place after a particularly heavy rainfall.

The *jowar* crop, both in the *kharif* and *rabi* season, has been seriously affected by only one disease, namely, the *jowar* smut, or *kani* as it is locally termed. No precaution against this is taken. In spite of the fact that the Agricultural Department has been recommending treatment of the seed with copper sulphate as a method completely successful in preventing this disease, and also of the fact that the Agricultural College is only six or seven miles away, not a single cultivator was met with who knew the treatment even by reputation. We hope that one of the results of our inquiries will be that the people will know of, and possibly adopt, the treatment.

As far as manuring is concerned, there is no regular treatment which is considered as necessary. A portion of the land receives house sweepings, ashes, and cattle manure every year, and sheep are folded on some of the *jowar* land during the hot weather (*see section on manuring*). The quantity of manure given is usually very small, say, not more than four cartloads or 1½ tons of manure per acre, even when it is applied at all.

The total weight of the crop per acre in the *kharif* and *rabi* seasons is practically identical, but the *rabi* crop gives more grain. The grain outturn varies from 300 to 500 pounds per acre per crop, and the straw or *kadbi* from 250 to 400 bundles of five pounds each. This latter yield is equal to 1,250 to 2,000 pounds per acre.

In an Indian cultivator's holding it is very difficult to judge the profit or loss where part or all the labour is supplied by the cultivator himself and the materials grown are largely consumed by him, his family, and his stock. We will, on the basis of information supplied by the villagers of this and other villages, endeavour to frame a statement as to the expenditure considered requisite on the one hand if all labour has to be paid for, and, on the other, if all the labour is that of the cultivator himself and his family. The former represents the cost of the work to a capitalist farmer; the latter that to a working cultivator. This will enable us to ascertain the money value of the average profit in growing the *jowar* crop in a village like Pimpla, and by the methods there adopted. The statement is for the *rabi jowar* crop, per acre, but the figures for the *kharif jowar* crop will be little different:—

	With hired labour.	With cultivator's own labour.
Expenditure.—	Rs. a. p.	Rs. a. p.
(1) Seed (8 pounds)	0 8 0	0 8 0
(2) Manure (4 carts at 8 annas per cart)	2 0 0	2 0 0
(3) Labour cost (animals and men)—		
(*a*) One ploughing	6 0 0	} 8 8 0
(*b*) Two harrowings	1 4 0	
(*c*) Sowing and covering ..	1 0 0	
(*d*) After cultivation	0 12 0	
(*e*) Watching	2 0 0	
(*f*) Harvesting, tying and stacking	2 0 0	
(*g*) Threshing and winnowing ..	1 2 0	
(4) Assessment	2 0 0	2 0 0
Total Rs. ..	18 10 0	13 0 0

Income.—	Rs. a. p.
Value of grain (average 400 pounds at 12 seers per rupee)	16 0 0
Value of *kadbi* (300 bundles at Rs. 5 per 100)	15 0 0
Total Rs.	31 0 0

This shows a *nett* return to a capitalist farmer of Rs. 12-6 per acre in an average season : a working cultivator would obtain on the other hand a *nett* profit of Rs. 18 per acre.

In the case of *kharif jowar* it is stated that the cost would be less by about Rs. 4 as no ploughing is required. On the other hand the grain yield will be less and the profit practically the same.

So far as the people inform us, they consider that the difficulties in the growth of *jowar*, when put on suitable land, are simply the fear of insufficient or untimely rain, and the *kani* or smut disease. The latter would seem to be easily amenable to treatment.

G.—Bajri and Tur.

Next to *jowar* in importance as a crop in the village is *bajri*, (*Pennisetum typhoideum*) or bulrush millet which represents, of course, the alternative crop, specially adapted to lighter and shallower land, for producing grain and fodder. It is so frequently associated with *tur* (*Cajanus indicus*), or pigeon pea, that we may consider these two crops as grown in the village together.

Bajri is always, here as elsewhere, a *kharif* crop of poor soils, the richer soils being devoted to *jowar*, wheat, carrots, etc. It is usual to plough land for *bajri* in December, January or February, or even later, though very often, if not usually, ploughing only takes place once in two years on typical *bajri* land. The ploughing takes place after the *rabi* crops are harvested.

For one or two months after this, the ploughed land is allowed to remain exposed to the sun, but in April and May two harrowings are given. The first requires two or even three pairs of bullocks with the harrow, and the cultivator himself has to stand on the implement to secure the crushing of the clods ; one pair of bullocks is sufficient in the later ones. A third harrowing is given after the monsoon rain has come, and just previous to sowing. It is specially given to remove the weeds and is termed *dhabri.*

As a rule no farmyard manure, or in fact any manure at all, is available for the *bajri* crop.

As soon as the soil is fit for sowing after the first monsoon showers have come, *bajri* and *tur* are sown with a four-coultered drill. A bamboo tube (*moghan*) is drawn after the drill in the line of the fourth coulter, and *tur* seed is sown down this bamboo tube. The fourth row thus receives both *bajri* and *tur.* The covering is done by the light harrow termed *pharat.* When the land is very full of clods a plank is used instead of the *pharat,* but the latter is much preferred because it removes the weeds at the same time as it covers the seeds.

The amount of seed required per acre is four to five pounds of *bajri* and eight pounds of *tur.* The quality of the *bajri* seed can be judged by an examination of twenty-six samples in two series obtained from the cultivators who were sowing the crop. The average purity in the two series was 98.1 and 97.1 per cent., respectively, and the average germination was 87.2 and 82.5 per cent. on the two occasions. This gives a mean proportion of useful seed of 85.5 and 82 per cent. or an absolute mean of 83.7 per cent.

Only one sample contained weed seeds chiefly of a species of *Amaranthus.* The variation in quality was considerable, as the following table (taking both series together) shows :—

Useful seed.	Proportion of Samples with this Percentage.
	%
90 to 100%	31
80 to 90%	38
70 to 80%	31

The general average of the seed was lower than in the case of the *jowar,* and thirty-one per cent. of the samples gave less than 80 per cent. of useful seed.

The *tur* seed was not by any means equal. From an examination of fifteen samples, the average purity was 96 per cent. This gives a mean percentage of useful seed of 85.8. The only weed seeds found as impurity was *Ipomœa eriocarpa* and *Alysicarpus rugosus*, but these were frequent. Some of the seed was attacked by weevils. The variation in quality is shown in the following table :—

Useful seed.	Proportion of Samples with this Percentage.
	%
90 to 100%	67
80 to 90%	20
70 to 80%	7
40 to 50%	6

After sowing, the plants, both of the *bajri* and *tur*, appear on the fourth or fifth day. After two to three weeks, or when the crop is about nine inches high, the usual bullock hoe is worked in the crop with two pairs of bullocks, and two men. A second bullock hoeing may be given when the crop is eighteen inches high, but it is not usual, and then nothing more is done, except scaring birds, until it is ready for harvest.

The *bajri* crop flowers in early September, and it is ready for harvest at about the middle of October. Watching begins from the end of September and continues for three weeks, as the crop is very attractive to birds. It is harvested with a sickle, and usually by women,—is allowed to lie in the field for about two days, when bundles are made, and cocks, made of five bundles, are heaped in the field. After stacking either in the threshing yard or in the field, it is usually threshed after two or three months.

Threshing takes place generally in January or February. If the plants are of specially large size the heads are removed and threshed alone, but otherwise the whole plants are spread in the threshing yard. Treading by bullocks is, of course, universally used for threshing. The grain is then winnowed by the wind in the usual way, a west wind being preferred to one from the east. The treading of the heads after removal of the winnowed seed is repeated three and sometimes four times to get the last portions of the seed. Beating with a wooden block is sometimes done instead of the fourth threshing.

The clean *bajri* seed is stored usually in bamboo baskets made nearly airtight by coating with cowdung and mud. The threshed straw and husk is kept and fed to cattle, chiefly in the monsoon. When the *bajri* crop is removed the *tur* remains in the field. At the time of the *bajri* harvest the *tur* plants are beginning to flower and are usually ready for harvest early in December. The plants are taken when the pods show signs of drying, being cut with a sickle and left to dry in the field for two days. The dry plants are bound with ropes of agave fibre, and taken to the threshing yard.

Some time later, these bundles are opened, the plants arranged with the tops all in one direction, and the seed is beaten out by hand with a piece of wood termed a *mogri*, the plants being laid on a wooden block on the ground. The remaining seed is then removed by treading with bullocks, and the united grain is winnowed by wind as usual. The husk of the seeds is somewhat valuable, and is carefully stored for feeding. The stalks are either burnt or used to support roofing tiles, or for making brushes for sweeping floors.

Bajri is not subject to any serious pests or diseases at Pimpla. *Tur* is liable to be attacked by wilt, which often affects a few plants in a plot. The caterpillar known as the pod borer is fairly common, and does considerable damage. Nothing whatever is done against these pests and diseases.

The yield of crop per acre varies much according to the distribution of the rain in the growing season. A good year will give an average of five measured maunds of *bajri* grain per acre, a bad season will give only two and a half maunds. The *tur* provides about sixty to seventy pounds of grain per acre. About four hundred bundles of *bajri* straw will also be produced, but it is relatively poor fodder.

Taking, as we did in the case of *jowar*, the case when all labour and bullocks have to be paid for, and all produce is sold, on the one hand, and, on the other, when the labour is the cultivator's own, the following may be considered an average statement of accounts for this crop, as estimated by the people. A man's wages are taken at 5 annas per day and the cost of a pair of bullocks at 10 annas per day :—

	With hired labour.	With cultivator's own labour.
	Rs. a. p.	Rs. a. p.
Expenditure.—		
Seed (5 lbs. *bajri*, 8lbs. *tur*) ..	0 9 0	0 9 0
Manure (nil)	....	....
Labour Cost		
(*a*) One ploughing	6 4 0	6 15 0 (items *a*–*f*)
(*b*) Two harrowings	0 15 0	
(*c*) Sowing and covering ..	0 7 6	
(*d*) After cultivation	0 7 6	
(*e*) Watching	0 15 0	
(*f*) Harvesting *bajri*, tying, stocking, threshing and winnowing	3 8 0	
Assessment	1 0 0	1 0 0
Total Rs...	14 7 0	Rs. 8 8 0
Income.—		Rs. a. p.
Value of *bajri* grain (average 420 pounds at 14 seers per rupee)		15 0 0
Value of *tur* grain (average 64 pounds at 12½ seers per rupee)..		2 8 0
Value of *bajri* straw (average 400 bundles)		3 0 0
Value of *tur* husks, etc.		1 0 0
Total Rs.		21 8 0

This shows a *nett* return to a capitalist farmer of Rs. 7-1-0 per acre in an average season: a working cultivator would, however, obtain a nett profit of Rs. 13-0-0 per acre. The chief point in which this crop is inferior to *jowar* is in the value of the straw. In any case *bajri* straw is inferior to *jowar*, but the manner of threshing reduces it to a bad condition for keeping and feeding. Perhaps the greatest criticism of the management of this crop is the badness of the threshing and winnowing. *Bajri* has to be threshed four times and winnowed thrice before it is clean. Surely this is not incapable of improvement, but no really satisfactory method has yet been devised and shewn to the public.

H.—Carrots and Peas.

This mixed crop is rather a special cultivation of Pimpla Soudagar and of the surrounding villages, and its popularity depends largely on the fact of a demand for the produce in the Poona market, and also on the fact that a good return can be obtained with little attention after once the crop is sown. Forty years ago, according to the people, wheat was their only money crop. When the cultivation of carrots was introduced a few years ago it was found to be less affected by the precarious character of the rains than wheat. Our village apparently was the pioneer in the growth of carrots, but its cultivation is now being taken up slowly by other places in the neighbourhood.

The carrots are grown on medium black soil, and the crop never receives any manure. The land is ploughed once every year after the rains set in and is harrowed twice or thrice. One acre is ploughed in two days and costs about six rupees, while two harrowings cost ten annas.

The crop is generally rotated with wheat or *jowar*, but some cultivators, very occasionally, grow it year after year for three or four years. It is almost invariably grown mixed with peas which form a minor crop, although a plot here and a plot there may be seen without the mixture of peas.

Although carrots are grown extensively at Pimpla the seed is always brought from Narayangaon, a village forty to fifty miles away. The seed grown at Pimpla does not apparently give as good a crop as the seed from Narayangaon. The growing of seed in the neighbourhood of Poona is not a paying proposition in any case.

The seed is bought at the rate of six to eight pounds a rupee. About forty pounds of seed are required for one acre. The seed for the peas, which can be had at the rate of about sixteen pounds per rupee, is also brought from Narayangaon. The seed rate for peas as a minor crop with carrots is fifteen to twenty pounds. The sowing season is from the end of August to the end of September. The carrot seed is broadcasted by hand either early in the morning before sunrise or in the evening after sunset. The reason given is that if the carrot seed is sown in the sun the carrots do not get the same good red colour as they otherwise do. Peas are sown by means of a four-coultered drill on the same day as the carrots or on the following day, and the land harrowed once.

Generally the cultivators divide their fields into two or three plots which they sow at an interval of about two weeks so that they can harvest the crop without much difficulty in getting the necessary labour.

There is no interculture. The crop is a dry one and is not irrigated. Only in exceptional cases where the cultivators have good wells the crop gets irrigation water at intervals of two to three weeks. If the crop is irrigated once then it must be irrigated all throughout, otherwise the yield is poor. The carrots grown under irrigation are said to be less sweet than the carrots without irrigation.

The peas germinate in about six days and begin to yield pods for marketing in about two months. The plucking of pods goes on for three to four weeks. The outturn of peas per acre is about two hundred and forty pounds. The green pods are taken in baskets to the Poona market and sold at the rate of twenty to thirty pounds a rupee.

The carrots germinate in about ten days and are ready in about four months when the leaves begin to turn yellow. The carrots are hand-dug, their leaves cut and the carrots are washed and carted to the Poona market. Digging and washing of one cartload of carrots costs about nine annas if the labour is paid for. The charge for carting to Poona is one rupee per cart. The yield is ten to fifteen carts per acre. Each cart, containing about six hundred pounds, fetches three to five rupees. Good selected carrots are used as vegetables but a large quantity of the produce is employed for feeding horses. The leaves of the carrots form a good fodder for the bullocks of the cultivators. The leaves of one acre are sufficient for six bullocks for one day.

The average cost of the crop and the returns expected from it per acre are shown in the following statement :—

	With hired labour.			With cultivator's own labour.		
Expenditure.—	Rs.	a.	p.	Rs.	a.	p.
Seed (carrots Rs. 5, peas Rs. 1-4)	6	4	0	6	4	0
Manuring	1	0	0	1	0	0
Labour cost (men and animals)—						
(*a*) One ploughing	6	0	0			
(*b*) Harrowing	0	10	0			
(*c*) Sowing and covering ..	0	10	0	15	4	0
(*d*) Plucking peas and digging carrots	13	0	0			
(*e*) Carting carrots to market.	15	0	0			
Assessment	2	0	0	2	0	0
Total Rs...	44	8	0	24	8	0

	Rs. a. p.
Income.—	
Value of carrots in market	45 0 0
Value of peas	10 0 0
Value of fodder..	2 0 0
Total	Rs. .. 57 8 0

The *nett* profit to a capitalist farmer is not large, amounting to only Rs. 13 per acre, but to a working cultivator it yields the very good return of Rs. 33-0-0 with very little outlay for expenditure in growing the crop. It will be seen that except for the cost of harvesting and of carting to market it is a cheap crop to grow. If the cultivator has a cart of his own which cannot otherwise constantly be employed, and if his family can be employed largely for the plucking of the peas and the harvesting of the carrots the net money return is excellent, and the fact that Rs. 55 per acre can be obtained in actual cash largely accounts for the popularity of the crop.

I.—Wheat.

The decline of wheat cultivation in the village of Pimpla Soudagar is perhaps the most striking agricultural change which has taken place in the last thirty years. We have already touched on the reasons for this but the matter may be discussed perhaps in more detail here. The people give three chief reasons for the abandonment of wheat cultivation. These are—

(1) Want of sufficient late rain.

(2) Want of fodder and increasing demand for fodder.

(3) The sub-division and fragmentation of land.

With regard to the first of these points—the want of late rains—the opinion of the people is definite. They state that the risk of planting wheat, even when the previous rainfall has been good, on the not very retentive medium black cotton soil of Pimpla is too great to allow it to be done now, whereas formerly this was not the case. It is not that the total annual rainfall is too small or is even declining; the complaint is simply of the rainfall in October, November, and to a less extent in December in recent years.

We feel that there is a considerable amount of justice in their contention. We may consider that with a *rabi* crop like wheat, on medium black soil, there should be at least 2½ inches of rain in October, 1 inch of rain in November and, perhaps, half an inch in December (although this last is less important) to secure a first class crop. How far this has been supplied in recent years as compared with those of twenty years previously is indicated by the following statement of rainfall for fourteen years previous to 1890, and for fourteen years previous to 1914 in Poona. We take Poona as the nearest place for which accurate records are kept and published :—

	Rainfall 1877-1890.			Rainfall 1901-1914.			
Year.	October.	November.	December.	Year.	October.	November.	December.
	Ins.	Ins.	Ins.		Ins.	Ins.	Ins.
1877	2.95	1.90	..	1901	2.78	..	..
1878	6.18	0.33	..	1902	3.80	0.49	3.15
1879	0.87	1.78	..	1903	3.89	..	..
1880	4.02	0.89	..	1904	6.66	..	..
1881	4.04	0.35	..	1905	2.52	0.34	..
1882	1.13	3.21	0.01	1906	0.60	0.40	0.02
1883	12.89	1.49	..	1907	0.57	0.04	..
1884	10.47	0.07	2.25	1908	0.70	0.75	..
1885	3.79	1.95	1.30	1909	1.63	..	..
1886	12.22	1.42	0.75	1910	5.22	2.83	..
1887	3.00	3.06	0.09	1911	0.25	2.50	0.19
1888	3.54	1.13	..	1912	8.41	2.84	..
1889	7.12	..	..	1913	1.37	..	..
1890	3.85	7.74	1.92	1914	0.83	0.86	0.02

It will be seen that in the years previous to 1890 the minimum limit we have suggested for rain in these months was exceeded—

(1) in October, 12 times out of 14, or in 86 per cent. of cases.
(2) in November, 9 times out of 14, or in 60 per cent. of cases.
(3) in December, 4 times out of 14, or in 29 per cent. of cases.

In the years from 1901 to 1914 a different state of affairs was shown. The minimum limit was only exceeded—

(1) in October, 8 times out of 14, or in 57 per cent. of cases.
(2) in November, 3 times out of 14, or in 21 per cent. of cases.
(3) in December, once out of 14, or in 7 per cent. of cases.

We may take the chance of getting satisfactory weather to produce a good crop to be indicated by the mean of the figures for October and November, ignoring those for December which are confessedly of less importance. A good crop in the fourteen years previous to 1890 would therefore probably be obtained in 75 per cent. of occasions; in the fourteen years from 1901-1914, it would probably have been only obtained in 39 per cent. of the years. The chance of an unsatisfactory crop or of a total failure is nearly twice as great, therefore, in recent years as it was previous to 1890.

Whether this is a cyclic variation, and a period when wheat will again be a suitable crop will come, we do not know, and it could in any case be hardly discussed here. The change during the last twenty-five years is, however, as clear as any such changes can be, and the cultivators seem to be quite right in their contention that the rain has become less suitable for wheat grown without irrigation.

The second reason given for the decline of wheat is the need for fodder, of which wheat gives very little and that of an inferior quality. In former days, when a fairly good crop of wheat could be looked forward to with confidence, a cultivator could sell the wheat and purchase other fodder. When the wheat crop could not be relied upon, the position of a cultivator was lamentable. He had not produced fodder himself and the crop on which he relied to purchase fodder had failed him. This could not go on, and he had perforce to turn his attention to a crop which would certainly provide a certain amount of good fodder. In this explanation the special need for a crop giving fodder seems again to be the result of the deficiency of late rain in recent years.

Thirdly, the sub-division of land is unfavourable to wheat cultivation. Wheat requires high cultivation, and the small holders cannot keep the number of bullocks and other moveable capital which are essential to the standard of cultivation needed for wheat. Further, when holdings become smaller it becomes impossible to allot a part of such holding to a fodder crop for cattle and a part to a grain crop such as wheat. It then becomes imperative that the crop grown should supply both grain and fodder and hence the replacement of wheat by *jowar,* though the latter does not place the same actual cash in the hands of the cultivator himelf.

The result which has followed from the operation of these and other causes is that while, according to the people, formerly nearly half the cultivated area of the village or, say, 300 to 350 acres was occupied by wheat, and wheat and gram formed the favourite rotation, now the area under wheat in 1914-15 sunk to 54 acres.

The reduction in the area under wheat in this village is no isolated occurrence. The district round Poona comprised in the Haveli taluka shows a reduction, which if not so great as that found in Pimpla Soudagar, is very considerable. The area under wheat in the Haveli taluka at different dates was as follows :—

1885-86	14,467 acres
1890-91	16,648 acres
1895-96	9,754 acres
1900-01	6,212 acres
1905-06	7,665 acres
1910-11	8,437 acres
1911-12	5,721 acres
1912-13	6,382 acres
1913-14	7,587 acres
1914-15	7,550 acres

We need not consider the year 1900-01 as this was affected by famine, but in any case there seems to have been a reduction to less than half the normal area before 1890. In 1890-91, moreover, wheat formed 6.6 per cent. of the cereal acreage: in 1912-13 it only forms 3.2 per cent. This reduction both in the absolute and proportionate acreage under a crop like wheat is a matter for serious consideration.

The chief varieties of wheat sown at present in the village are three in number:—

(1) White-awned variety.
(2) Awnless variety.
(3) Black-awned variety.

The first of these is of old standing in the village, and does not seem to have had any special name until recently when the name *pandra kusal* was given to distinguish it from the black-awned variety more recently introduced. The awnless variety was obtained, according to the people, by selection of occasional awnless plants which appeared in the fields, and although other samples of seed have now been obtained from other villages like Chinchvad, the basis was local selection. The black-awned variety was only recently introduced either from Chinchvad or from the Agricultural College at Poona.

In growing the wheat crop few peculiarities are noticed in this village. The land is ploughed in June or July and is then harrowed two or three times at intervals of from eight to fifteen days. The value of deep ploughing and good tillage for wheat is fully recognised, but it is not always possible to give it, especially when the cultivator does not possess his own cattle and implements. As a rule the manure produced by the cultivator's own cattle and house, and which is not used for making dung cakes, is applied by preference to the wheat crop. The amount applied may reach eight to ten cartloads or, say, 6,000 to 8,000 pounds of manure per acre in alternate years. Sheep folding is often practised on wheat land, say, once in three or four years. The actual cost of manuring does not annually amount to more than Rs. 2.

No further tillage is done till after the so-called *hasta* rains at the end of September or beginning of October, when the seed is sown with the four-coultered drill termed *moghan*. This is heavy, and ensures the seed being put in up to six inches deep, in rows six to eight inches apart. The land is then gone over with the *pharat*. The seed rate is forty to fifty pounds per acre. The wheat crop is always sown alone. The seed used was found to be of high quality giving an average purity of 97.8 per cent. and an average germination of 94.6 per cent.

After sowing, no further attention is given till harvest. There is no interculture. In exceptional cases one or two irrigations with water are given in November but this is not usual. In January or February the crop is ready for harvest. It is cut close to the ground with a sickle and at once tied into sheaves. These are allowed to dry, if necessary, before heaping together. It is considered by the people better to harvest before the grain is quite hard, as the wheat is then stated to give a better yield of flour.

Wheat is not affected by any diseases except rust and, occasionally, smut.

The threshing is done, as usual, under the feet of bullocks, and the winnowing in the wind. The grain is stored for sale in bags or baskets smeared with cowdung. Seed for the following year's crop is usually mixed with ashes and kept in baskets sealed with cowdung.

The yield of an average crop per acre is from 350 to 450 pounds of grain and 200 bundles of straw. It varies, of course, very much indeed according to the amount and the timeliness of the rain.

Taking, as with previous crops, the case when all labour and bullocks have to be paid for, and also when the cultivator supplies the labour, the following may be considered an average statement of accounts for a fairly good wheat crop, as estimated by the people. A man's wages are taken at 5 annas per day, and the cost of a pair of bullocks at 10 annas a day:—

	With hired labour.	With cultivator's own labour.
	Rs. a. p.	Rs. a. p.
Expenditure.—		
Seed (40 pounds, at 12 pounds per rupee)	3 5 0	3 5 0
Manure	2 0 0	2 0 0
Labour cost—		
(*a*) One ploughing	6 4 0	
(*b*) Two harrowings	1 4 0	
(*c*) Sowing and covering with *pharat*	1 6 6	7 13 0
(*d*) Harvesting and preparation for market	2 0 0	
Assessment	2 0 0	2 0 0
Total ..	18 3 6	15 2 0
Income.—	Rs. a. p.	
Value of wheat grain (450 pounds, at 16 pounds per rupee) ..	28 2 0	
Value of wheat straw (This is an estimate simply, for the wheat straw is never sold).	2 0 0	
Total..	30 2 0	

The profit then, calculating on the above basis, would be Rs. 11-14-6 per acre, or, say, Rs. 12 to an employer, and Rs. 15

to a working cultivator. This is not high in either case, but with the exception of the value of the wheat straw, the whole is a cash receipt, and hence wheat is considered as a money crop by the people of the village. It is, evidently, a far more valuable crop, however, for a capitalist employing labour than for a cultivator. The proportion of labour in the total cost of the crop is small, and a cultivator can get a much bigger return by growing a crop like carrots which demands more labour. This, as well as the reasons previously discussed, has, we believe, something to do with the relative decline in the popularity of the wheat crop.

J.—Gram.

Intimately associated with the cultivation of wheat is that of gram, (*Cicer arietinum*), for it has generally in the past been considered as the natural rotation crop with wheat. Its position in the cropping scheme has risen and fallen with the latter. At present it must be considered as a crop whose importance varies very much from year to year. On the whole, however, it usually occupies a far smaller area than it did twenty years or more ago. This fall in the area of gram with that of wheat is illustrated not only in Pimpla Soudagar but also in the taluka in which it is situated. The correspondence is not exact, but it is close enough to be striking :—

	Average area under wheat.	Average area under gram.
1885-86 to 1889-90	13,513	7,858
1890-91 to 1894-95	11,056	8,286
1895-96 to 1899-00	7,190	6,099
1900-01 to 1904-05	8,098	6,559
1905-06 to 1909-10	7,902	3,886
1910-11 to 1914-15	7,135	4,334

The fall has been similar in the case of the two crops. Its progress has not coincided, but there is at least enough correspondence to suggest the intimate connection between the growth of the two crops in the part of the country round Poona, as is certainly stated by the people at Pimpla Soudagar.

In Pimpla, at present, the soil usually taken for wheat, namely, a medium black soil of fair depth with a *murum* substratum, is not taken for the crop. The lighter *mal* lands, considered as suitable for *bajri*, are more usually employed, and gram is taken in succession to that crop. The system here is to take a *kharif* crop of *bajri* and then if enough moisture remains in the soil, a gram crop is tried. The crop is, however, never expected to give very much return.

The preparation of the soil in this case consists only in removing the stubbles of the previous *bajri* crop, if any, followed by the sowing of the gram crop by the drill. Nothing more is done. The land is neither ploughed nor thoroughly harrowed and no after-tillage is given. Manure is never applied to gram.

The cultivator, in fact, sows the gram crop in the early part or middle of October, and then does not return again to the field until February to harvest the crop. Usually he finds the crop is very poor. In 1914-15 one cultivator drilled 36 pounds of seed and got 15 pounds of gram! The seed used was found to be good, yielding 94.5 per cent. of useful seed. The only weed impurity consisted of a few seeds of *Alysicarpus rugosus*.

The seed rate is generally from 32 to 40 pounds per acre. When the crop is good, it is said to be 400 pounds but this quantity is rarely obtained.

Thus cultivated, an actual statement of accounts in connection with what would be a normal good crop per acre is given below:—

	Wth hired. labour.	With cultivator's own labour.
	Rs. a. p.	Rs. a. p.
Expenditure—		
Seed (40 pounds)	2 0 0	2 0 0
Manure	....	....
Labour cost—		
(*a*) Cleaning up previous crop or harrowing	0 14 0	
(*b*) Drilling and covering seed ..	1 0 0	2 0 0
(*c*) Harvesting	1 8 0	
Assessment	1 0 0	1 0 0
Total	6 0 0	5 0 0
Income—	Rs. a. p.	
Value of grain (400 pounds, at the rate of 20 pounds per rupee) ..	20 0 0	
Total	20 0 0	

The profit here shown (Rs. 14 per acre for a capitalist or Rs. 15 for a working cultivator), is hardly ever obtained. The yield given is what a man hopes for and what he may get once in a generation.

It would be a mistake to consider this catch crop growth of gram on lighter black soil or on *mal* land as in any way representing gram cultivation in the Poona district. It is a local development under the special conditions, for gram cultivation as generally done is a very different operation, and the crop represents really in most places one of the paying crops of Deccan agriculture.

K.—NIGER SEED.

One of the commonest crops of the drier and shallower land of the Bombay Deccan is niger seed (*Guizotia abyssinica*), generally called *til*, or *kala til* by the people. The term *til*, in fact, in the neighbourhood of Poona, among the cultivators, means niger and not sesamum as it does elsewhere in the north of the Bombay Presidency. It occupies a relatively large area, not because it is particularly profitable, but because it will grow with little attention in the lighter and shallower land of the village, not being attacked by animals or by other pests.

We have little to say about this crop, as the cultivation and attention given to it is very small. Land even too poor for *bajri* and *tur* will do for niger seed. No ploughing is given but three or four harrowings instead. The first of these is given in February and the next a few days afterwards to break up the clods. No manure is applied. The seed is sown with a four-coultered drill early in the rains at the rate of four pounds per acre. The seed used was somewhat variable but good on the whole. One sample contained seeds of *Commelina forskalii* as an impurity, while the average amount of useful seed was 86 per cent. No other crop is grown in admixture with niger. The land is hoed once, later, when the crop is a few inches high. No watching is necessary, and it ripens about the same time as *bajri* or a little later.

The time for cutting is when the seed capsules are fairly dry but not too dry, as in the latter case the seed falls. The cut plants are allowed to dry in the field for a day or two, are then bound with grass ropes, being carried in large bundles to the threshing yard. If the stalks are thin the whole plants are trodden out as usual by bullocks ; if they are stout then the plants are beaten by hand. In the former case the husks and stalks can be eaten by cattle ; in the latter they are usually burnt as fuel. The seed is winnowed and stored as described for other seeds.

The yield obtained is, in good cases, from 160 to 240 pounds per acre. Anything under one hundred and sixty pounds is considered a poor yield. The accounts for a niger crop at Pimpla are, on an average, as given by the people, as follows :—

	With hired labour.	With cultivator's own labour.
Expenditure.—	Rs. a. p.	Rs. a. p.
Seed (2 seers)	0 4 0	0 4 0
Labour cost		
(*a*) Harrowing	0 15 0	1 12 0
(*b*) Drilling and covering ..	0 7 6	
(*c*) Hoeing	1 0 0	
(*d*) Harvesting	1 0 0	
Assessment	0 12 0	0 12 0
Total ..	4 6 6	2 12 0
Income.—		
Value of seed produced (160 pounds)	Rs. a. p. 8 12 0	
(The husk and stalks have no market value.)		
Total	8 12 0	

The nett return is therefore very small, not more than about Rs. 4 to Rs. 4-8 on the average for a capitalist or Rs. 6 for a working cultivator. A good crop of 240 pounds would only bring a nett return of about Rs. 13 or Rs. 18 per acre, respectively, under the two conditions quoted. It must be remembered, however, that the land devoted to this crop is the poorest in the village which is cultivated at all.

L.—Groundnut.

Considered in point of area, groundnut is a very minor crop but it is nevertheless one of some interest, because of the attitude of the people towards it, and the possibilities which it possesses for the future.

The history of groundnut in the village, as told by the people, is the same as it has been in other parts of the Deccan. It is said to have been formerly cultivated to a considerable extent, but the country variety, which was then grown, demands late rain in order to ripen. Failure of late rain meant failure, and so the crop gradually disappeared. The introduction of foreign varieties,—Spanish and Japanese,—has caused a revival of the cultivation which, however, so far shows little sign of extending. These varieties ripen in less than five months, and it is found that they can be relied upon to give a crop. At the present time *no* country groundnut is grown at all ; its cultivation has entirely disappeared. The usual variety is that known as " Big Japan."

On the whole, however, the cultivators consider that carrots and peas form a better paying crop than groundnut, and that it is doubtful whether *rabi jowar* is not more profitable. This is, of course, a direct result of the nearness to a good market to which the alternative crops can be sent, at which fodder and vegetables always fetch a high price.

For groundnut the heavier and deeper black soil is avoided, because it becomes sticky in the rains, hard after the soil dries, and forms very heavy cracks when the rains are over. All these characters are unfavourable to the crop. The medium black soil is preferred, more particularly in fairly lowlying places where moisture may be expected to be retained. The use of the smallest types of groundnut, which grow on less retentive light soils, is only just commencing.

The land is ploughed in March to six inches deep, the ploughing being often with four or even five pairs of bullocks. No attempt is made to cross plough—the only really effective method of securing thorough cultivation with the country plough. If the time is missed, ploughing is omitted and harrowing only takes place. Two harrowings follow the ploughing at intervals of eight to fifteen days, and the land then remains ready till sowing time. Sowing is not done until the soil is wet to a depth of nine inches, when a light plough is driven over the land and the groundnut dibbled in the furrow by women. The rows are from eight to nine inches apart. The *pharat* is used to cover the seed. The seed is usually obtained from the Agricultural College farm, Poona, and is sown at the rate of seventy to eighty pounds of seed per acre. At present, as already stated, " Big Japan " seed is the favourite.

The crop is hand weeded once. No further attention is given until harvesting and no irrigation is employed. The digging of the nuts is done by women, who are usually paid in kind. If cash payment is given, the rate is from two to two-and-a-half annas per day. The harvesting takes place in November.

Two difficulties are met with in growing groundnut. The first is that, immediately after planting, all the birds of the neighbourhood, particularly crows and pigeons, seem to visit the fields and dig up the seeds which have been sown. With all the care which is given a good many of the seeds disappear, and we do not remember to have seen a field of groundnut which was anything like filled with plants. The other enemy of groundnut is the *ticca* disease of the leaf, which always appears to a small extent, but has not been found serious with the early-ripening foreign varieties. These difficulties are those generally found in groundnut growing in the Deccan and are in no way peculiar to this village.

As a rule no manure is given to groundnut in Pimpla. Sometimes five to ten cartloads of farmyard manure per acre or some household sweepings and ashes are applied once in two years. In a few cases, among the wealthier cultivators, sheep folding is practised, say, once in three or four years on groundnut land, not with the idea of specially benefiting this crop, but as a general treatment to keep the land in good condition.

If the plots of groundnuts are small, the produce is generally used for home consumption: otherwise in this village the green nuts are at once put in bags and carted to Poona market. In Pimpla Soudagar the nuts are not dried to any extent—the nearness of Poona making it more profitable to sell them in the fresh condition. The average outturn of green nuts is from 1,800 to 2,250 pounds per acre. The green creepers are fed to the cattle and are considered a very good fodder.

A statement as to the estimated cost of and return from a well-cultivated crop of groundnut in Pimpla is as follows:—

	With hired labour.			With cultivator's own labour.		
	Rs.	a.	p.	Rs.	a.	p.
Expenditure.—						
Seed	10	0	0	10	0	0
Manuring (estimated proportion) ..	2	0	0	2	0	0
Labour cost—						
(*a*) Ploughing	6	0	0			
(*b*) Two harrowings	1	4	0			
(*c*) Sowing and covering seed ..	2	12	0	9	12	0
(*d*) Weeding and harvesting ..	15	0	0			
(*e*) Carting to market, including octroi	4	0	0			
Assessment	2	0	0	2	0	0
Total ..	43	0	0	23	12	0
Income.—						
Value of 2,080 pounds of green nuts (65 maunds of 32 lbs. at 12 annas per maund)				Rs. a. p. 48 12 0		
Value of green creepers				2 0 0		
Total ..				50 12 0		

The *nett* return is thus only Rs. 7-12 per acre for a man who works with hired labour. It must be remembered that a large part of the cost is represented by labour, and so for a cultivator who uses his own and his family's work the return is much better and will reach about Rs. 27 per acre. Moreover, the seed will usually be his own produce and will have actually cost much less than the amount specified, and the manuring will generally mean only the cost of carting the material to the field unless sheep folding is used.

M.—Peas.

We have already dealt with peas as a subordinate crop to carrots. It is, however, of sufficient importance as a separate crop to merit attention, especially as its cultivation is one of the characteristics of the village.

Peas are grown on medium black soil, which is only manured with a little farmyard manure once in three or four years, while sheep are folded on this class of land at intervals. The land is ploughed once and harrowed twice, and the seed sown, as usual, with a four-coultered drill after the rains set in, at the rate of 40 to 50 pounds per acre. The seed is almost always brought from Narayangaon near Junnar, as this has the reputation of being particularly good. It appears above ground about six days after planting.

The plot is usually hand-weeded once, three weeks after sowing, and then again ten days later. The crop of peas is sold green in the Poona market, and the first picking is usually ready two months after planting. Crops are obtained for about six weeks, that is to say, until the end of September. The yields of these pickings per acre are, on the average :—

First picking	..	..	125 pounds.
Second picking	..	..	250 pounds
Third picking	..	..	200 to 250 pounds.
Fourth picking	..	..	200 to 250 pounds.
Fifth picking	..	..	100 pounds.

Each picking requires four or five women per acre for a day, each paid 2 annas.

When they first come on the market at the beginning of August, peas fetch a rupee per ten pounds in the Poona market. This price rapidly drops to half (twenty pounds per rupee) or even to one-third (thirty pounds per rupee). The cost of carrying in baskets to Poona market is three annas per twenty-two pounds. When the crop is finished the vines are pulled out and used as fodder for cattle.

The land devoted to peas is used for *rabi jowar* or wheat or sometimes even gram, after the peas are removed—one of the few instances of double cropping in the village.

A statement of expenses and returns per acre from this crop as estimated by the people, is as follows :—

	With hired labour.	With cultivator's own labour.
	Rs. a. p.	Rs. a. p.
Expenditure.—		
Seed	3 0 0	3 0 0
Manuring	1 0 0	1 0 0
Labour charges—		
(*a*) Ploughing	6 0 0	5 8 0
(*b*) Harrowing	0 10 0	
(*c*) Sowing and covering ..	0 10 0	
(*d*) Hand weeding (twice) ..	2 8 0	
(*e*) Picking (five times) ..	3 2 0	
(*f*) Carrying to market ..	2 10 0	
Assessment (one-half debitable to this crop)	1 0 0	1 0 0
Total	20 8 0	10 8 0

	Rs.	a.	p.
Income.—			
Value of first picking (125 lbs.) at 10 pounds per rupee	12	8	0
Value of second and third pickings (350 lbs.) at 20 pounds per rupee	17	8	0
Value of fourth and fifth pickings (300 lbs.) at 30 pounds per rupee	10	0	0
Total	40	0	0

This shows a nett return of Rs. 19-4-0 per acre, but if the cultivator does his own work, it is subject to the same remarks as have been made in the case of groundnut, and will yield a *nett* profit of Rs. 29-8-0. The crop is therefore highly considered as one which brings a good deal of actual cash into the pocket of the cultivator who grows it, beyond any value as fodder possessed by the plants after removal of the peas.

N.—Sugarcane.

The only other crop which demands separate treatment is sugarcane, not because of the large area it covers, for it is only a crop occasionally grown and it never exceeds seven acres in area, but because it represents the typical intensive culture of the Deccan, which a cultivator is almost always anxious to grow if he has a good well and circumstances are favourable. The methods, however, are very different and less intense than on the irrigation canals only a few miles distant.

The soil used for sugarcane is that termed "medium black." The ploughing of the land begins by the end of January, and five ploughings are given with the country plough, with an interval of a week between the operations. The *pharat* is finally used to level the land and smooth the surface. During the ploughing about seventy-five cartloads of farm-yard manure per acre are incorporated with the soil.

The variety of cane grown is the large, thick, high-yielding cane of the district, known as "*pundia,*" and the seed is either taken from the previous year's planting or else bought from the canal irrigation tract. In one case mentioned to us the seed cane was actually brought from Nanded in the Nizam's Dominions. The cane is cut into sets about one foot long, each with about three eye buds. About 16,000 such sets are required per acre, and their cost comes to Rs. 80 for the sets and at least Rs. 15 for carting them to the village.

In March the land is ploughed for the sixth time, in order to prepare the furrows for planting the sets. Water is allowed to run into these furrows and the sets are then laid in the furrow and pressed into the soil by trampling. The land is irrigated after four days, and again after five days further. After this time, the cane is watered once every week, except when an adequate amount of rain is received.

The land is weeded for the first time a month after planting and, in all, three weedings are given. In July the furrows are split up and beds are formed and the crop is earthed up. Before earthing up, a topdressing of about 21 bags (of 80 pounds) of fish manure is given, costing about Rs. 75 per acre. The fish used contains from six to eight per cent. of nitrogen.

The harvesting and preparation of the *gul* or crude sugar are done when the cane is ripe in February or March, and are carried out exactly according to the Poona method. All operations are carried out by the village people, but almost the whole of the labour required has to be paid in any case. One acre of cane will give forty to fifty-five boilings, and each boiling gives two blocks of *gul* of seventy pounds each. The yield of *gul* is therefore from 7,000 to 7,700 pounds per acre. The trash and megass are used for boiling the juice and no fuel beyond this is required, except for the first pans of the season.

No ratoon crop is taken in this village, as experience has proved against its success.

With regard to the return yielded by sugarcane so cultivated, we have the following statement per acre :—

	With hired labour.			With cultivator's own labour.		
Expenditure.—	Rs.	a.	p.	Rs.	a.	p.
Seed (16,000 sets per acre)	80	0	0	80	0	0
Manuring—						
75 carts farmyard manure	112	8	0	112	8	0
21 bags fish manure..	75	0	0	75	0	0
Labour charges (men and animals)—						
(*a*) Ploughing	36	0	0	24	0	0
(*b*) Harrowing and levelling ..	1	2	0	0	12	0
(*c*) Planting	5	0	0	....		
(*d*) Weeding	10	0	0	....		
(*e*) Earthing up	8	0	0	....		
(*f*) Watering (30 waterings) ..	95	10	0	64	0	0
(*g*) Harvesting and preparing *gul* ..	60	0	0	60	0	0
Assessment	2	0	0	2	0	0
Total Rs. ..	485	4	0	418	4	0
Income.—	Rs.	a.	p.			
7,200 pounds *gul* at Rs. 18 per *palla* of 240 lbs.	540	0	0			

This shows a nett return of Rs. 54-12-0 per acre to a man working entirely with hired labour, and Rs. 121-12 for a working cultivator. The return, of course, stands far higher than that of any other crop in the village, but the necessary outlay is very large and usually has to be borrowed, and, moreover, the crop is on the land for almost a whole year. On the other hand, sugarcane is a very reliable crop if proper care is taken, and the risk of the market falling has been very small in the last eight or ten years. It will be seen that, cultivated as it is, a drop of ten per cent., or less than Rs. 2 per *palla*, would wipe out the profit for a man working with outside labour, and a fall of twenty per cent., or less than Rs. 4 per *palla*, would make it unprofitable for a working cultivator. On the other hand, any rise in price such as has been brought about by the European war, brings in a very large profit with this crop.

O.—Other Crops.

The other crops in the village are grown on a very small scale, present few features of interest, and affect very slightly the life and labour of the village. A few words with regard to them seem all that is required.

Rice has appeared in a very few recent years among the crops grown in the village, but on a very small scale, and simply in certain low lands into which water from the higher areas can be easily conducted. It is here grown without transplanting, the seed being drilled at the commencement of the rains and the crop reaped in October or November. It is considered here as a profitable but somewhat risky crop, being ruined by a long break in the rains, and also by the heavy downpours sometimes received during the ripening of the grain.

The other pulse crops consist of *kharif* crops [except *val* (*Dolichos lablab*) always grown in the *rabi* season] and present no features of interest. They usually give very small returns, but *kulthi* (*Dolichis biflorus*) is suitable for light shallow lands, and will give a crop when no other leguminous plant will grow successfully.

For the rest, there is nothing to add to what has already been said on pages 71 and 72.

P.—General.

We are now in a position to make an approximate calculation as to the nett return which the whole land of the village may be expected to give to a working cultivator. It is obvious that the figures given above for the nett profit for an average good crop are in most cases considerably higher than the actual profits obtained at present. The poorer land in the village of which there is very much (*vide* page 19) yields very much less than the amount given, and even with those crops to which good land is usually devoted, there is always a considerable acreage which, owing either to inferior cultivation or the attacks of pests and diseases, yields less than the amount suggested. We shall not be making too great a deduction if we count that the acreage under the *jowar*, *bajri*, *bajri* and *tur*, gram, wheat and miscellaneous pulse crops, will yield, on the average, twenty per cent. less profit than that indicated in the previous sections, and that the carrots, peas, and groundnut will yield at least ten per cent. less. For sugarcane outside labour is always employed, and the nett profit cannot be put at more than Rs. 100 per acre. We shall thus have for the total profits yielded to the village by the area under the various crops in 1915-16 as follows :—

Crop.	Area.	Profit per acre.			Total profit for village.		
	Acres.	Rs.	a.	p.	Rs.	a.	p.
Jowar	346	14	8	0	5,017	0	0
Bajri and Tur*	79	10	8	0	679	0	0
Rice	6	16	0	0	96	0	0
Wheat	55	12	0	0	660	0	0
Peas	41	26	8	0	1,086	8	0
Other pulses..	54	10	0	0	540	0	0
Carrots and Peas	78	29	8	0	2,301	0	0
Other vegetables	7	10	0	0	70	0	0
Niger seed	68	6	0	0	408	0	0
Groundnut	9	24	0	0	216	0	0
Sugarcane	7	100	0	0	700	0	0
	750				11,823	8	0

* The whole of the *bajri* is not cultivated with *tur*, but we have taken the profit when not with *tur* as Rs. 2 less per acre. The error is probably slight.

This gives an average profit per acre for the whole village of Rs. 15-7 if we include the extra large area of sugarcane in 1915-16. If the area of this crop be normal (as on the average of the last three years), then if we take Rs. 14-8 as the amount usually obtained by a working cultivator on the whole cultivated land of the village, the result will probably not be far out. If it errs at all, it places, we think, the return a little too high.

It might be at once asked as to whether this return per acre would be increased in a dry village like the present, either by changing the character of the crops or by improving the methods of cultivating them, without very considerable out-of-pocket expense which would be beyond the powers of the cultivators to incur. In answer, we would say that there is no doubt that such improvement could be made, as judged by the results given at the agricultural college farm only five to six miles away. Cleaner, better cultivated land has consistently given much higher returns, the use of green manuring has, with practically no cost except that for labour, been a great success in increasing the yield of the staple *rabi* crops, the most serious disease of the *jowar* crop, exceedingly abundant in this village, has been entirely eliminated at a cost of one or two annas per acre, and the introduction of new crops, like cotton, in this area has led to vastly improved returns. But under the land conditions described in the previous chapters improvements like these are very slowly admitted into the village. When once introduced, however, by one of the leading successful cultivators of the village, they spread like wild fire.

It is this sort of thing which produces the sudden and rapid changes in the cropping which the records show, which has led to what is undoubtedly the most successful feature of the cultivation in the village, namely, the growth of carrots and peas for the Poona market, and which at the same time presents a very strong barrier of conservatism against other undoubted improvements.

CHAPTER V.

The Agricultural Stock of the Village.

The Deccan is not in any sense an area for keeping and breeding stock. The black soil does not grow good grass, and on the *murum* and other lighter lands the grass herbage is very poor. In a few places, where waste lands abound, or where the facilities of fodder and water are particularly good, large numbers of cattle are kept, and sheep and goats are pastured during part of the year. But, with all this, the animals are relatively few, are chiefly kept for actual use, and it is only when one gets to the margin of the Deccan that one reaches what may be termed typical breeding tracts.

During the hot weather, that is to say, in March, April, and May, large flocks of sheep and goats are kept in this and the surrounding villages. They are fed on the leaves and shoots of *babul* and other trees together with such other herbage as they can pick up, and they belong to wandering *dhangars* or shepherds. These drive them about the country, and are paid for allowing them to stay for a day or two on the fields of cultivators in order to manure the land. The average amount charged by the *dhangars* per day for the folding of a hundred sheep on a piece of land is fifteen pounds of grain or about Re. 1.

The actual number of animals in the village belonging to the people in the spring of 1914, when our census was taken was as follows :—

Cattle	.. ..	226
Buffaloes	.. ..	58
Goats	.. ..	11

Beyond this there is a very small number of fowls.

PLATE X.
(*To face Page* 116.)

Some of the Village Animals at Pimpla Soudagar.
(*This view also shows something of the general type of house.*)

These animals are very well distributed among the people of the village. Out of the 111 families of which the village is composed, 70 possess cattle or buffaloes and five in addition have only goats. 39 families have both working and milking animals (cattle and buffaloes), 21 have only milking animals, and 10 have only working cattle. Thus 67 per cent. of the village households have animals of some sort belonging to them. Not only this, but no family has more than seven working animals, or six milking animals, and the highest number of both adult cows and buffaloes owned by one household is 13.

Milking Animals.—In Western India the animals kept for milk are usually buffaloes. The cows are looked upon chiefly as breeders of working bullocks, and only incidentally as milking animals. In all cases, both of buffaloes and cows, the calf, if alive, is allowed to suck milk from the mother before milk for use or for sale is taken, and this must be taken into account in judging the quantity of milk given by the animals.

The animals used for giving milk number sixty cows and thirty-six buffaloes or ninety-six in all. The relative number of milch and dry animals in March was as follows :—

	In milk.	Dry.	Total.	Percentage dry.
Cows ..	36	24	60	40 per cent.
Buffaloes ..	22	14	36	39 per cent.

The number of dry animals seems excessively high.

All the cows are of the ordinary Deccan breed, and all the buffaloes, except four, are also of the Deccan type. The four remaining are of the Surti breed and are of a much better milking type.

The quantity of milk given by the animals, after allowing the calf to suck, was very variable. Among the buffaloes the highest amount was seven pounds per day, while several gave six pounds per day. The average amount obtained from the buffaloes was only four pounds per day. Among the cows the quantity was still smaller, the maximum being three pounds, and the average only two pounds per day. No wonder, if these figures are common, that the cow is hardly considered as a commercial milk-yielding animal in the Deccan! The buffalo yields more, double the quantity or more in fact, and though its yield is still exceedingly small, it is at least more a commercial producer of milk than the cow.

The daily estimated yield of milk in the village was 88 pounds from buffaloes and 72 pounds from cows, or a total of 160 pounds. The bulk of this is used in the village, but a variable quantity is sent to Poona market by two or three of the village producers. At the time of our animal census (1914) only 23 pounds were sent to Poona: when we made our house census, the quantity was about 120 pounds and the actual amount varies very much according to the local demand and according to the season.

The way in which this milk is sent to Poona is generally by hand. Sometimes a small single-bullock cart is kept to take it, but, as a rule, it is taken by loads of about twelve pounds per person, and carried on the head, about seven to eight miles. The man or woman not only conveys it to the city, but also delivers it, or disposes of it, and receives six annas per day for the work. This amounts to a charge of about half an anna per pound of milk.

The milk is often watered before being sent to Poona, and is still more often watered before being sold. Analyses of samples intercepted on their way to Poona market gave figures as follows :—

	Cow's Milk.		Buffalo's Milk.	
	I%	II%	I%	II%
Total solids ..	11.0	10.7	14.4	14.4
Fat	4.5	4.2	6.2	6.6
Solids not fat	6.5	6.5	8.2	7.8

Both classes of milk show decided signs of watering, but the buffalo's milk nevertheless remains a fairly good milk. The cow's milk is, on the other hand, shamelessly watered, and this watering has been thus done in the village before the milk was despatched. The price obtained for the milk in Poona City varies, and the producers frankly confessed to us that they suited the quality to the price offered. The normal price expected for unwatered milk in Poona is one rupee for not more than 12 pounds.

The milk not sent to Poona is used in the village. At the time of our census there were twenty gymnasts under training who took 30 pounds of milk per day, but this was a special circumstance. Leaving this aside, it may be stated that at the time (March 1914) there was available 107 pounds of milk for a population of over five hundred, including over 150 children. The quantity per head of population is thus very small, in fact, only about 3 ounces.

Working Animals.—At the time of our census there were 105 working animals in the possession of 49 families. These are all bullocks, though the bulls (of which there are three) may occasionally be used for work. All are used for agricultural purposes, or for carting when the season does not demand the work of the bullocks on the land. This provision of animals gives about one pair of bullocks per twenty acres of assessed area. Carting brings in about Rs. 1-4 per day when the cart can return to the village at night.

All the working bullocks are of the ordinary Deccan type and demand no remark.

Feeding of the Cattle and Buffaloes.—The public grazing area in the village is very small—only 4¼ acres for 284 animals. But they spend their time in getting what they can from the boundaries of fields, from the stubbles in the fields after removal of the crops, and from the uncultivated and fallow area where a little grass fodder grows. All such unoccupied land is enjoyed in common by the whole of the village cattle.

Beyond this the usual feed of the cattle is *jowar* or *bajri* fodder, with carrot tops and pea fodder when available. This is usually all that is given to the young stock, to bullocks that are not working, to cows not in milk, to the bulls, and to any others not yielding immediate returns. For milking animals and working animals, oilcake is given up to an amount of about two pounds per day. The cake is almost always safflower (*kardi*) or niger seed cake, or a cake made from a mixture of these two.

Housing of Cattle.—There are no sheds specially built for cattle in the village, and the animals are tied either on the verandahs of houses, or actually inside the rooms. The floors of these places is usually only soil, or at most *murum,* and freely absorb urine and other excreta. The space per animal depends on circumstances, and if an owner has several animals it may be very small.

The cattle dung is removed and collected daily, but the urine is always wasted. During the greater part of the year, that is, for about eight months, most of the dung is turned into dung cakes for burning on the banks of the river. These are the chief fuel of the village, but about forty tons are sent to and sold in Poona, where they bring about Rs. 15 per ton. In the rains this method of utilisation is impossible, and the dung is then collected in numerous manure pits just outside the village site, and afterwards utilised for the crops. An account of these is given in another chapter.

The dead bodies of the village animals belong to the *mahars* of the village, who eat the flesh and sell the hides.

Value of Animals.—The price of cattle has been going up very much in recent years, and there is no doubt that the agricultural stock forms a very important part of the village assets. At present we estimate the actual money value of the stock in the village as follows :—

	Rs.	a.	p.
105 bullocks at Rs. 60 per animal	6,300	0	0

	Rs.	a.	p.
3 bulls at Rs. 90 per animal	270	0	0
36 cows in milk at Rs. 40 per animal	1,440	0	0
24 dry cows at Rs. 15 per animal	360	0	0
58 calves at Rs. 8 per animal	464	0	0
22 she-buffaloes in milk at Rs. 60 per animal ..	1,320	0	0
14 she-buffaloes dry at Rs. 20 per animal ..	280	0	0
22 buffalo calves at Rs. 5 per animal	110	0	0
11 goats at Rs. 4 per animal	44	0	0
Total	10,588	0	0

The stock forms thus a very important part of the village assets.

CHAPTER VI.

THE PEOPLE OF THE VILLAGE.

WE have so far considered the village land, the way in which the land is held and cultivated, and the agricultural stock held by the people; it now remains to investigate the character of the people, their caste, their material condition and, in general, the manner of life which results from the conditions in which they are placed. This we have done so far as the circumstances allowed, and we now venture to present the data we have obtained and the conclusions we draw from them.

The village, as already stated, is a small one, and from a recent house to house census which we have made, it contains 111 families and a population of 556. By far the largest number of the people are Marathas by caste, and among these nearly all are related in some degree to one another. The actual castes to which the families belong are as follows :—

(1) Marathas	93
(2) *Sonar* (goldsmith)	1
(3) *Sutar* (carpenter)	1
(4) *Ramoshi* (watchman)	1
(5) *Chambhar* (shoemaker)	1
(6) *Mahars*	10
(7) *Mangs*	3
(8) Mohamedan	1
	111

The whole of the non-Maratha population are, in fact, official village servants, and entitled to some share in the *baluta* or charge against all the crops grown, for services rendered each in his separate sphere. The work of all these village servants, except the last three, has been already indicated. Of these three, certain of the *mahars* in rotation are officially the village messengers and the general servants of the village *patel* or headman for village purposes. They put up the tents of visitors to the village, carry money to the treasury, act as guides to strangers, clear away dead cattle and other refuse, and so on. For doing this they have their own land which they hold under an *inam* tenure (see p. 36 and 37), they enjoy a portion of the *baluta* which is obtained from the cultivators, and they have the right to the carcasses of dead animals in the village. They are the most numerous class of village servants. The duty of the *mangs* is to furnish ropes for all agricultural purposes which they make from the fibres of several local plants and particularly from the agave which abounds in the neighbourhood. They also work as general labourers, and their women spend a good deal of their time not only in making ropes, but also in preparing baskets, brooms and matting, largely from the leaves of the *shinde* or toddy palm. The solitary Mohamedan family so often found in Maratha villages is a butcher. Marathas are flesh eaters, at least occasionally. They object, however, to kill the goats required, and so a Mohamedan is kept in the village for the purpose, and receives a share of the village *baluta*.*

Of the castes mentioned, the *chambhars*, *mahars* and *mangs* are considered untouchable and live in a separate *wada* or group of houses outside the village site. The *ramoshi* is considered as little above them in status.

The village, like all ryotwari villages, is under the control of the *patel* or headman who is in charge of whatever happens, and is responsible to, and is a paid officer of, Government. In most villages the duties are divided between two village officers, the *mulkhi patel* responsible for the general control of the village, and the police *patel* responsible for the detection and prevention of crime and for keeping peace in the village; in a small place like the present, one man does both

* The real reason, perhaps, for the presence of a Mohamedan butcher is not a prejudice against killing, but rather that in the high Maratha families there has crept in, we know not how, a feeling that flesh before being eaten must have been blessed by the *munjawar* or priest of the local Mohamedan saint or *peer*. We are indebted to H. H. The Chief of Ichalkaranji for drawing our attention to this point.

duties. Beyond this there is the village *kulkarni*, generally a Brahmin, and in the case of small villages like the present, acting as accountant and collector of Government revenue for a group of villages. In the present case the incumbent of this office lives at Aundh, three miles away, and is responsible for the accounts of five villages beside the one with which we are dealing. It will thus be seen that the village consists essentially of Marathas, with village servants of other castes, and it is governed by Marathas.

The total population, as we have already stated, is 556, of whom 459 are Marathas. In obtaining data with regard to this population, we may say that we have counted as men and women those who, on an approximate calculation, exceed sixteen years of age. Those below that age are considered as children, boys or girls as the case may be. This age was taken because in the Indian social system a young man, and especially a young woman, practically takes on the full duties of an adult at little more than this age,—and moreover in calculating the requirements for living in the way of food and clothing one must, in any case, consider those older than sixteen as essentially adults. All married girls living with their husbands are counted as adults. Taking this limit we find the people in the village are as follows :—

Caste.	No. of families.	Total population.	Men.	Women.	Boys.	Girls.
Marathas ..	93	459	159	161	76	63
Sonars (goldsmiths) ..	1	3	1	2	..	..
Sutars (carpenters) ..	1	3	1	1	1	..
Ramoshis ..	1	11	3	5	2	1
Chambhars ..	1	6	1	3	1	1
Mahars ..	10	50	16	20	8	6
Mangs ..	3	20	12	7	..	1
Mohamedans ..	1	4	2	1	..	1

From these figures we see that in this typical Maratha village we have as follows :—

(1) The Marathas themselves form 82.5 per cent. of the whole population. Of the rest, 14 per cent. are composed of the depressed classes (*chambhars*, *mahars* and *mangs*), while all others only reach 3.5 per cent. in number. A Deccan village of this type is, therefore, a very homogeneous community, and except for the essential distinction and separation between the untouchable classes and the rest, the caste system hardly affects the village at all.

(2) The number of members per household is exactly five. At first sight this would seem a very satisfactory state of affairs, and one very different from that found among certain classes of the community previously investigated by one of us under Indian city conditions.* But owing to the fact that many of the families are joint, and also to the fact that boys of sixteen years old and over have been counted as adults, it is difficult to draw definite conclusions with regard to the size of each individual family. Making all allowance for the method of computation, it appears, however, that the presence of only 161 children below the age of sixteen in 111 households represents a very unsatisfactory state of affairs. The data available do not seem to justify any very definite conclusions on the subject, but they make one suspect that the population has reached almost a stationary condition, if it is not actually declining.

(3) The relative number of males and females calls for little comment. There is a slight excess of females among the adults (which might be expected as married girls are always counted among adults), and a slight but very small excess of males on the whole population.

The housing of this population is astonishingly good. Practically all the houses, even those of the depressed classes, are built of stone, which is not remarkable as stone abounds in the village. They are, on the whole, of good size, and the average house area per household is about 200 square

* H. H. Mann: *The Untouchable Classes of an Indian City.* "Sociological Review," 1912.

feet. The figures for house area were obtained from eye observation at the time of taking our house to house census. Naturally there is considerable variation as the following table shows :—

Size of house.	Number of this size.
Over 1,000 square feet	1
From 500 to 1,000 square feet	8
From 200 to 500 square feet	27
From 100 to 200 square feet	33
Under 100 square feet	42

In spite of the fact that there are some very small houses the housing here is much better than is usually found in Indian villages, even in the Deccan.

Labour.—In an ideal agricultural village, under the ryotwari tenure, the whole population would be engaged in one or other way in connection with the cultivation of the land or in serving the needs of those who are connected with the land. We have departed very far from this condition of things here where a very considerable proportion of the households have members who either wholly or partially do other work, most of them acting as labourers either in Kirkee (five miles away) or elsewhere. The numbers and occupations of these in the spring of 1916 were as follows :—

	Marathas.	Depressed classes.	Others.	Total.
(1) Working in Ammunition Factory, Kirkee ..	62	24	3	89
(2) Employed in carrying milk to Poona and selling it there	9	..	1	10
(3) Carting on the roads, chiefly with their own carts ..	4	..	..	4
(4) Artisans	2	..	2	4
(5) Labourers	14	..	..	14

Of the artisans one was a gardener, one a bricklayer, and two were stone quarriers. Of the labourers one was engaged at Government House, Ganeshkhind; two were women. Three of them were temporarily in Bombay, but have been included in the village population.

The large amount of village labour engaged in the ammunition factory, Kirkee, is undoubtedly abnormal. Many of those there engaged would, under more normal conditions, have been engaged in carting, in ordinary labouring work, or would have remained at home in the village. All those there engaged are, however, men and boys, and it is rather astonishing to find that, out of a male population of 283 no less than 89 (or 31.4 per cent.) should be able to leave for such work, and should be content to do so. Of course, the off season from an agricultural point of view (when this census was taken) is a very unoccupied time in a village consisting, like the present one, essentially of dry cultivation, but it represents probably the maximum labour available at present for work elsewhere if the attractions are sufficient to draw the men and boys away from the village.

Perhaps the waste of labour at present is best illustrated by the number of people engaged in carrying milk to Poona City (eight miles away) and delivering it there daily. Each conveys about six seers (twelve pounds) per day, and the greater part of the day is occupied. The pay per day is about six annas. Thus ten people are employed to carry and deliver 120 pounds of milk, at a cost of Rs. 3-12 per day. The charge seems very high per pound of milk (½ an anna) but the striking feature is the waste of labour, for one man could certainly take and deliver this and a great deal more, if provided with a one-horse conveyance, and the cost would certainly not be more than that now paid.

Carting on the roads, when it is in the neighbourhood of the village and the cart can be brought back to the village at night, as for instance, when a cart is engaged to go to Poona and back, is paid for at the rate of Rs. 1-4-0 per day. This means practically six annas per day for the man, twelve annas per day for the pair of bullocks. The actual return to the man is practically a labourer's wage.

*Total Village Income.**—On the basis of the material which we have described in considering the crops, we have attempted to calculate the income for every family in the village. In doing this it must be recognised that the result is an approximate one as it is based on a number of assumptions, the chief of which are as follows:—

(1) The average return to a cultivator, working himself on the land, is Rs. 14-8 per acre of cultivation. This will, of course, vary very much according to the class of land, but if we consider the village as a whole, the result will not differ very widely from the truth. The method of arriving at this figure has been described in a previous chapter.

(2) It has not been necessary to make any assumption with regard to the average wage of a labourer working outside or inside the village, as we have the actual amounts received in practically all cases. It is usually six annas per day for service outside the village for an adult man, and four annas per day for work inside the village. Women's labour is three annas outside and two annas inside the village.

(3) We have calculated that a landholder who rents his land to a cultivator receives Rs. 7 per acre, and that a cultivator gets, on the other hand, Rs. 7-8 per acre. This is an average amount which we have fixed after many inquiries.

(4) There are two items which we have not been able to apportion to particular families, and have only attempted to calculate for the village as a whole. These are first the return from fruit trees—mango and tamarind,—and from babul trees for timber. The two former of these have been taken as Rs. 2-8 per mango tree per annum and Rs. 2 per tamarind tree per annum. The second item is the return for manure cakes which are constantly made on the river bank during

* By this term we mean the total income of every family in the village added together.

the greater part of the year by women, and then carried to the Poona market. We calculate that in the year no less than eighty tons of these are made in the village (half of these being sold in the Poona market) and that the return in money is no less than Rs. 600 per annum.

Our returns are not quite complete, and the figures presented only take account of 103 out of the 111 families in the village. The income from the fruit trees and the manure cakes just described is, therefore, slightly too high when calculated per family, but the error introduced is very small; we have, in fact, as follows :—

Total income of 103 families ..	Rs.	21,450	per annum.
Income from fruit trees and babul ..	Rs.	409	per annum.
Income from sale of dung cakes ..	Rs.	600	per annum.
Total ..	Rs.	22,459	

This, it will be seen, works out at Rs. 218 per family or an annual income per head of population of Rs. 43-3-0. It must be realised that these figures have been obtained by converting income from *baluta* (of which more later, considered under expenditure) into money value at the *nett* village rate, and that in each case it is income as considered from a family's own point of view.

The proportion of the income of the 103 families derived from land and from other sources is as follows :—

From land	Rs.	7,947
From other sources	Rs.	13,503
Proportion from land ..	37.0	per cent.

The calculation of the income of the families of the village is comparatively easy when one is in close touch with the families themselves, and when reliable assumptions are made regarding the return available from land. It must be recognised, however, that the return assumed is that obtained in an average good year. A year when the rain fails puts the calculation all out ; and when, as we shall see, there is little or no reserve capable of being saved in good years, the result will spell disaster.

Village Expenditure.—When one turns to try and compute the necessary expenditure of the people of the village under ordinary normal conditions in order to form a balance-sheet and so judge the present economic position of the village, we are met by many difficulties. But we have been able to form some idea of what is considered by the people as their necessary expenditure, according to the condition of indebtedness, and hence of interest, which has grown up.

Debts of the Village.—In trying to do this we will first consider the indebtedness of the village and the annual charge on this account. Our figures relate to 103 families as in the calculation of income, and so represent probably somewhat less than the actual indebtedness of the village as a whole.

The total amount of indebtedness of these 103 families in the village is Rs. 13,314. Of this, Rs. 5,819 is on landed security, and Rs. 7,495 is on personal security.

So far as debts made on landed security are considered, these are now officially recorded, and without official registration the bond cannot be easily enforced. The mortgage bonds are of three types. These are—

(1) *Najar Gahan*, or ordinary mortgage, in which the land is still held and worked by the debtor on his own account. Under this heading 35 acres are mortgaged by four people for Rs. 2,900, or nearly Rs. 83 per acre.

(2) *Tabe Gahan*, or mortgage, in which the land is handed over to the creditor, but can be redeemed on repayment of debt and interest. Under this heading 34 acres are mortgaged by eight people for Rs. 1,530, or Rs. 45 per acre. In the case of one holder the same piece of land was also mortgaged under the third heading. One of these only has been considered in the final calculation.

(3) *Mudat Kharedi*, or deferred sale, in which, if the loan is not repaid within a definite period, the lenders automatically

takes possession of the land. Under this heading 19 acres are mortgaged by seven people for Rs. 1,699, or Rs. 89 per acre.

The total amount of money involved was obtained as to Rs. 1,204 from seven local village people, as regards the rest it was advanced by money-lenders (*sawkars*) in Poona and elsewhere.

The amount advanced on land, however, represents much less than half the total indebtedness of the village. The remainder was lent on the personal security of the borrowers—who are recognised as substantial land-owning cultivators—on the understanding that dealings for the sale of crops and the purchase of supplies shall be through the lender. This, of course, is a general method in India, and this village probably represents the condition of things which would prevail almost all over the Deccan.

The rate of interest varies much. It is never less than 12 per cent., often 24 per cent., and sometimes even as high as 72 per cent. The portions of the money at various rates of interest were as follows :—

On Land.—

At 12 per cent.	Rs.	4,619
At 18 per cent.	Rs.	200
At 24 per cent.	Rs.	1,000
	Rs.	5,819

On Personal Security.—

At 12 per cent.	Rs.	1,525
At 18 per cent.	Rs.	1,320
At 24 per cent.	Rs.	3,200
At 36 per cent.	Rs.	1,210
At 54 per cent.	Rs.	40
At 72 per cent.	Rs.	200
	Rs.	7,495

The average rate of interest on money raised on land is 14.3 per cent., of that raised on personal security is 23.4 per cent. The average rate for the whole indebtedness is 19½ per cent., and involves an annual payment for interest of Rs. 2,592. As we shall see later, this payment for interest on debts is a crushing burden on the present village, and amounts to an annual charge of about 2.3 per cent. on the present capital value of the place.

Expenditure on Balutas.—In the organisation of a ryotwari village in the Deccan, as we have already noted, the village servants are paid by an annual charge against the crops which are grown, which every cultivator must give. The amount is termed *baluta.* The actual amount is a fixed amount of grain and fodder on the crops grown for grain and fodder; on the other crops it is nominally a similar charge; in the latter cases, however, it is commuted for a quantity of grain and fodder to cover what is supposed to be the due amount—but this introduces an indefiniteness into the whole, which makes it difficult to find out exactly what is given. By comparing the account of the transaction given by the receivers of the *baluta* and by those on whom it is charged, we have got the following as the approximate amounts recorded by those to whom it is due:—

	Annual Baluta.	
	Grain in pounds.	Bundles of *Jowar* fodder.
(1) *Ramoshi* or watchman	1,920	1,000
(2) *Sutar* or carpenter	1,920	1,000
(3) *Navi* or barber	1,920	1,000
(4) *Chambhar* or shoemaker	960	500
(5) Ferryman (at the river across the road leading to the village) ..	480	250
(6) *Mahars* (see above)	480	250
(7) *Mangs* or ropemakers	240	125
Carried forward ..	7,920	4,125

Brought forward ..	7,920	4,125
(8) Mohamedan butcher	240	125
(9) *Parit* or washerman	120	60
(10) *Gurao* or priest of the temple ..	120	60
(11) *Koli* (provides water to officers coming to the village)	120	60
(12) *Sonar* or goldsmith	60	30
	8,580	4,460

To ascertain what this means it will be wise to convert these quantities into the average money value. Taking grain as being worth 24 pounds per rupee, and the bundles of fodder as being worth Rs. 4 per 100 bundles, the total value comes to Rs. 536. This sum compared with the value of the produce for the cultivated area of the village (Rs. 14-8 per acre, *vide* page 114) comes to between 9 pies and one anna per rupee of income from cultivation. In our following calculations we have taken it as 9 pies in the rupee throughout.

It may be well to pause here to consider what is the normal average *compulsory* burden on the land of the village. This consists of the Government assessment, the local fund cesses, and these *balutas* which are part of the organisation of the village and which none can escape. We have thus :—

Government land assessment, —average per acre assessed	Rs.	1.63
Local cesses, average per acre	Rs.	0.10
Balutas, average per acre assessed	Rs.	0.52
Total ..	Rs.	2.25

We shall see later that the capital value of the land is not greater than Rs. 80 per acre, and thus the annual compulsory charges amount to 2.8 per cent. on the capital value.

Personal Expenditure.—In order to get an idea of the economic position of the people of the village it is necessary to get an accurate idea of the standard of life which they themselves consider necessary. Such a standard is difficult to obtain among those who do not keep accounts, but we have made many inquiries, direct and indirect, and have been able to fix what may be considered as a minimum standard, below which it would be considered that a self-respecting family cannot go. As for food, the amounts given are considered necessary to maintain efficiency; as regards other things, including clothes, they are what is required to maintain self-respect.

The calculations have been made for a family of five persons, composed of one man, two women, and two children.

Food.—For such a family the following supplies are considered necessary. It will be noticed that no extras are allowed for, no meat is provided and the ration given may be considered as a minimum. The prices are the nett village prices of the materials produced on the land, which would, within the past two or three years, have been obtained by the village people when acting as sellers.

Material.	Quantity required per annum.	Value per annum.		
		Rs.	a.	p.
(1) *Bajri* and *jowar* grain (24 lbs. per rupee)	192 lbs. per month .. =2,304 lbs. per annum.	96	0	0
(2) Rice (12 lbs. per rupee)	48 lbs. per annum ..	4	0	0
(3) Pulses (16 lbs. per rupee)	80 lbs. per annum ..	5	0	0
(4) Wheat (12 lbs. per rupee)	48 lbs. per annum ..	4	0	0
(5) *Gul* (sugar) (10 lbs. per rupee)	30 lbs. per annum ..	3	0	0
(6) Salt (24 lbs. per rupee)	48 lbs. per annum ..	2	0	0
(7) Chillies (6 lbs. per rupee)	24 lbs. per annum ..	4	0	0
(8) Oil, spice, etc.	.. ..	24	8	0
	Rs.	142	8	0

Thus the minimum cost for food for a family of five persons, such as we have described, is Rs. 142-8, or Rs. 11-14 per month. If we count a woman as requiring four-fifths and a child as three-fifths the food of a man, the necessary expense for food will come to Rs 37-8 per man, Rs. 30 per woman, and Rs. 22-8 per child, per annum. Considering the wages paid, these amounts may appear high, but we doubt whether they are so. They account for the anxiety to get the women of the family to work as much as possible, and for the children of the family to work as soon as possible.

We do not attempt here to discuss the relationship of such a ration as that just described with a theoretical necessary standard of life. It simply is a statement of what is actually considered necessary by the people themselves.

Clothing.—On the question of the amount of clothing necessary the people are very vague indeed. The general consensus of opinion was, however, that a man or woman would each require Rs. 12 per annum to appear respectable according to village standards. A child would require half this on the average. There is little doubt, however, that a saving is made in this item when the income is short.

Other Expenses.—For rent we have calculated nothing. The house and the land on which it stands almost invariably belongs to the man occupying it, and though an annual charge on the necessary original expenditure ought to be made, yet it is not an out-of-pocket expense, except in so far as it is included in interest charges. The annual repairs are represented by labour only. Beyond this we have taken other expenses to be about Rs. 5 per Rs. 100 of income. This amount is spent for household needs, such as brass pots, other utensils, soap, kerosene oil, and other things. Where used, tobacco and liquor come under this heading, but the village we are discussing happily does not possess a liquor shop, and the nearest is at Chinchvad, between two and three miles away. The amount, too, includes expenditure for holidays, which chiefly consist in visiting fairs in connection with temples, and other religious festivals. The estimate is low, and if money is available it will, undoubtedly, be exceeded.

The expenditure per family and per man, woman and child considered necessary by the people themselves is thus as follows:

	Man.			Woman.			Child.			Family of 5 persons.		
	Rs.	a.	p.	Rs.	a.	p.	Rs.	a.	p.	Rs.	a.	p.
Food ..	37	8	0	30	0	0	22	8	0	142	8	0
Clothing ..	12	0	0	12	0	0	6	0	0	48	0	0
Other expenses (counting total income as Rs. 200-0-0) ..	....			....			....			10	0	0
										200	8	0

Seeing that the average family consists, as has been already seen, of five persons, it would appear that, after paying all interest charges on debts and after payment of all *balutas*, each village family should have an income of Rs. 200 per annum if it is to maintain itself. In other words, the *nett* income per family in the village should be of this amount.

This (Rs. 200-8-0) represents the *nett* income which a family of five persons (one man, two women, and two children) would require if it is to maintain itself, after payment of all *balutas* and all interest charges on debts. The *actual* amount required by the *actual* family in this village will be a little more, namely, Rs. 212-2-0, as the proportion of adults is greater than in the ideal family for which the calculation was made. This gives Rs. 42-14 per head, on the average for the 103 families for whom our records are complete.

In the case of those families, who, as they cultivate land, must pay *baluta*, the minimum necessary income must be higher. These amount to 71, and pay Rs. 380 per annum, or an addition of Rs. 5-10 to the necessary income. We thus have :—

71 families with a necessary income of Rs. 212-2-0+

Rs. 5-10-0, or Rs. 217-12-0 per family of average size, or almost exactly Rs. 44-0-0 per head.

32 families with a necessary income of Rs. 212-2 per family of average size, as they pay no *baluta*, or Rs. 42-14 per head.

Balance Sheet for Village.—On the basis of these conclusions we are now able to draw up a balance-sheet for the village, or rather for the 103 families for which our data are sufficient. The total income of these families, calculated family by family, is Rs. 21,450. To this we have to add, for the village as a whole, Rs. 409 for fruit and other trees, and Rs. 600 for manure cakes made in the village. This gives a grand total of Rs. 22,459. This amounts to Rs. 218 per family* or almost exactly Rs. 44 per head. This clearly indicates that for the families paying *baluta* the income is on the average just sufficient to meet the expenditure, while for the others there is a slight excess of income. It seems to indicate that the people of the village can pay for their own maintenance, can pay compulsory Government charges on the land, and other compulsory charges on the land. There will be, however, nothing over in the case of the landholders, and very little in the case of others.

The actual figures are as follows, referring, however, only to the 103 families for whom we have data :—

Income.†—

	Rs.
Income from land (p. 129)	7,947‡
Income from other sources (p. 129) ..	13,503
Income from fruit trees (p. 128) ..	409
Income from manure cakes (p. 128 & 129)	600
Total ..	Rs. 22,459

* The number of souls per family for the 103 families is 4.95.

† The difference between this figure and that given on page 114 is due to the fact that a good many of the landholders and cultivators in this village actually live in adjoining villages, so that the total income from land does not correspond with the total produce of the village land, and also to the fact that this balance sheet only deals with 103 families.

‡ Government assessment is deducted from the income, and hence is not included in expenditure.

Expenditure.—	Rs.
Interest on debts (p. 132)	2,592
Necessary personal family expenditure* (p. 136 & 137)	22,501
Total .. Rs.	25,093

The figures show, thus, that if there were no debts the village, *considered as a whole,* should be just about able to pay its way if the seasons are good, if the amount of outside employment was always equal to that found in June and July 1916, and if each cultivator himself worked his own holding and paid no unnecessary outside labour.

The existence of debts alters the whole position. We have already discussed the amount of debt (see page 131) and the interest paid upon it. From the calculations just given it would appear as if in a village like the present there is hardly any money to pay interest on debts at all unless it be taken from what are usually considered as essential and necessary expenses to preserve efficiency and self-respect in the village. The amount, at the standard taken, available for payment of interest on debts for the whole village would be *nil.* The debt charge per annum, however, as we have seen, is Rs. 2,592, and the balance must be found, if found at all, from the amount which ought to be allowed for the necessary items of personal expenditure.

In working this out we have intentionally calculated on what is considered as an average good crop on the land. If such a crop is not obtained, then the position will be correspondingly worse. It is stated by the people that such a full average crop is only reached at the most in two out of three years. So that even at present it would seem that the economic position of the village must be steadily deteriorating.

So far, we have calculated for the village as a whole. As the families represented in the village are not all in the same

* This includes Rs. 536 paid by 71 families as *baluta.*

economic position, it becomes important to find what proportion of the village is in a satisfactory, and what proportion is in an unsound, economic condition. In order to do this we have divided the population into three classes, as follows :

(1) Those families in which the income derived from land is alone sufficient to maintain them in a sound economic position.

(2) Those families in which the income derived from the land, together with that from outside labour, is sufficient to maintain them in a sound economic position.

(3) Those families in which the economic position is unsound even when income from land and from outside labour are both considered.

The numbers in each class are as follows :—

(1) 8 families.
(2) 28 families.
(3) 67 families.

It thus appears that out of 103 families investigated, only 36, or just under 35 per cent., can pay their way on the standard they themselves lay down. The others are living below that standard—and this conclusion, which seems very clear, forms an exceedingly serious state of affairs.

It may be useful if we attempt to examine a little more closely the families belonging to each of these classes.

Group I.—The first group consists of eight families. All are landowners, but the families are small. Three consist of a single person, one of two persons, three of four persons, and one of eight members. The average number of members per family is hence very small, being only 3.1 persons. Counting all the adults as possible contributors to the family income we have the extraordinary position of 19 members out of 25 being possible money-earners. This accounts without much more study for the present satisfactory economic position. Let the number of children increase, and most of these families would fall into Group III until the children earned money, when it might stand in Group II. The amount of land held in this group (8 families) at present is 126½ acres, or almost exactly 5 acres per head. In only two families is the land income supplemented by outside labour, so that the land remains essentially the source of livelihood.

But the most striking feature of the records of these eight families is the absence of debts. Only two families are recorded as being in debt, and their indebtedness only amounts to Rs. 450, all bearing interest at 12 per cent. The interest charge is only 4.3 per cent. of the total expenditure.

The general position of this group is shown by the following figures for the eight families :—

Income.—		
From land	Rs.	1,699
From outside labour	Rs.	232
Total	Rs.	1,931
Expenditure.—		
Personal Expenditure (including *balutas*)	Rs.	1,200
Interest on debts	Rs.	54
Total	Rs.	1,254

The factors which enable a family, not depending on the outside labour of its members, to rise to an independent position are evident. They are (1) the small size of the family, (2) a large proportion of contributors to the family income in the family and very few children, (3) the absence of debts.

Group II.—The second group is composed of all those who are able to pay their way either wholly or partially by means of money received for labour, either in or out of the village. It consists, as already stated, of 28 families. Of these eleven have no income from land, and the whole of their income is from wages for labour. The group consists of 21 families of Marathas, three families of *mahars*, and two families of *mangs*, while the village *sutar* and the village *ramoshi* belong also to this group.

The average number of members per family is higher than in the last group, and the average number is 4.85 persons. The actual numbers are very variable, and we have actually as follows :—

Number per family.	Families with this number
1	3
2	4
3	3
4	3
5	1
6	8
7	2
8	1
9	2
11	1

Again we have a very large excess of adults, that is to say, of possible contributors to the family income. There are 107 adults and only 30 children. The former amount to over 78 per cent. Again this fact largely accounts for the satisfactory economic position. If the number of children increased, most of the families would sink, temporarily, into Group III. The average amount of land held in this group (28 families) at present is 5.17 acres per family. As we have already said, only 17 families possess income from land, and hence these on the average hold 1.8 acres per head.

In regard to debts, the position is very different from that in Group I. Out of 28 families 24 have debts hanging over them and the indebtedness in the group amounts to Rs. 3,154. The interest on this money is Rs. 652 per annum, and amounts to nearly 9½ per cent. of the total necessary expenditure.

The general position in the group is shown by the following figures for the 28 families :—

Income.—

From land	Rs.	1,740
From outside labour	Rs.	6,710
Total	Rs.	8,450

Expenditure.—

Personal expenditure (including *balutas*)	Rs.	6,238
Interest on debts	Rs.	652
Total	Rs.	6,890

The factors which enable a family to maintain itself in a sound economic position in this group are (1) the large numbers of adults and hence of possible money-earners in the families, and (2) the very small number of children. The debts make it necessary to earn about ten per cent. more than the families need for their maintenance.

Group III.—The third is by far the largest group in the village. It consists of those who cannot pay their way and live according to the village standard, even when the earnings of those who work at Kirkee and elsewhere are counted. The group consists, as already indicated, of 67 families. Of these 14 have no income from land, and hence the whole of their income is wages for labour. The group consists of 56 Maratha families and seven *mahar* families, while one *mang* family, one *chambhar* family and the Mohamedan family belong to this group.

The average number of members per family is again higher than in Groups I and II, and the average number is 5.2 persons.

The actual number is very variable, and we have actually as follows :—

Number per family.	Families with this number.
1	1
2	4
3	11
4	14
5	8
6	8
7	7
8	1
9	3
10	1
18	1
19	1

In these families the excess of adults, though still marked, is not so great as in the former two groups. There are 239 adults and 113 children. The adults thus amount to just under 68 per cent. It is important to notice how the proportion of children increases as the economic position sinks. We have, in fact, for the three groups :—

	Per cent. of children.
Group I (solvent from land alone)	22 per cent.
Group II (solvent from land and labour)	
Group III (insolvent)	32 per cent.

The average amount of land held in this group (67 families) at present is 6.35 acres per family. Out of the total number of families only 52 families possess income from land, and hence these on the average hold 1.54 acres per head. There are 48 families paying *baluta* (amounting to Rs. 221), and 10 families receiving Rs. 100 on this account. Nine families have no interest in the *baluta* either as payers or receivers.

The position with regard to debts is considerably worse than that shewn in Group II. Out of 67 families 30 have debts hanging over them, and the indebtedness of the group amounts to Rs. 9,249. The interest on this money amounts to Rs. 1,809 per annum, and amounts to nearly $10\frac{3}{4}$ per cent. of the total estimated necessary expenditure.

The general position in the group is shown by the following figures for the 67 families:—

Income.—

From land	Rs.	4,899
From outside labour	Rs.	6,169
Total	Rs.	11,068

Expenditure.—

Estimated personal expenditure (including *balutas*)	Rs.	15,178
Interest on debts	Rs.	1,809
Total	Rs.	16,987

There is thus a deficiency per family of Rs. 88 per annum

There is one point which it is necessary to make clear. In this group it is *not* the debt, in spite of its large amount, which keeps the majority of this group in an insolvent condition. If the debt were entirely wiped away, only nine families out of 67 would be placed in a sound position. It would, of course, improve the position of the others, but still they would not be able to pay their way. Thus it would appear that no less than 58 families, or more than half of those in the village, are in an unsound economic position, even independent of the question of debt. It is obvious that this is a very important conclusion, if confirmed elsewhere. The provision of a sound, cheap system of credit would not place these on their feet. It would help the others undoubtedly, but the causes of the general position of the village lie deeper than the exactions of the money-lenders.

Summary of Groups I, II and III.—Thus an examination of the position of the three economic groups into which we have divided the village shows that the people in the most sound position are those with small families, with few children, with much land and with few debts. Only 8¾ per cent. of the families are able to maintain themselves on their land alone, 27 per cent. on land plus outside labour, and the remainder appear to be unable at present to reach the standard of maintenance which they themselves set up. As the economic position gets lower the size of family increases. Whether it is the size of family that drags a household down to a lower economic plane, or whether it is poverty that has something to do with the larger family, is not entirely clear in all cases. But it is evident that it is the absence of children, and the very large proportion of money-getters in the families, that keeps very many of those in Groups I and II in a fair economic position.

We have on the whole the following position :—

	Group I (Solvent from land alone.)	Group II (Solvent from land and labour.)	Group III (Insolvent.)
Number of families in group ..	8	28	67
Number of population in group ..	25	137	452
Income.	Rs.	Rs.	Rs.
(*a*) From land	1,699	1,740	4,899
(*b*) From labour, etc.	232	6,710	6,169
Total ..	1,931	8,450	11,068
Expenditure.			
(*a*) Personal and *baluta*	1,200	6,238	15,178
(*b*) Interest	54	652	1,809
Total ..	1,254	6,890	16,987
Excess (+) or deficiency (—) ..	+677	+1560	—5919
Excess or deficiency per family ..	+85	+56	—88
Excess or deficiency per head ..	+27	+11	—13

The amount of indebtedness increases with the lower economic position of a family, and while the relatively small indebtedness in Groups I and II is a great factor in keeping them in a sound position, yet the absence of debt would apparently do very little at the present time to restore the families in Group III to solvency. Nine families only out of sixty-seven would be placed in such a position by the absence of debt.

This economic enquiry into the condition of the people of a typical dry Deccan village is disheartening. The debts are a crushing load on the people, but even were they removed more than half the families would still not be able to pay their way, counting personal expenditure at their own standard. And this is the case when outside employment was particularly active, and when no less than 30 per cent. of the male population were employed at fairly good rates at Kirkee. In the absence of such active employment it would be necessary for a part of the population to desert the village and seek employment, say, in Bombay for part of the year at any rate, and in the end, almost inevitably to sever their connection with the land. We fail to see how this can be avoided even as it is, unless the land can be made to yield more than it does at present, or unless the local rate of wages increases.

The latter of these changes is going on, though hardly faster than the actual increase in the cost of living. The former, *i.e.*, the increase in yield from the land, has hardly begun. We will speak of this again in the final chapter, but at present it seems a most urgent need that very serious attention should be devoted to meet the situation which the data recorded in this chapter reveal, if indeed the maintenance of the condition of the people should be the principal aim of the ruling powers.

CHAPTER VII.

General Conclusions.

We have now indicated the results of our inquiries into the life and labour of the people of a typical dry village in the western Bombay Deccan. It remains to try and estimate the relationship of the various economic factors to the actual capital value of the village, including the property belonging to its people—provided this can be even approximately ascertained—and then to summarise the conclusions which we can draw from our study.

The actual capital value of the village and the possessions of the people—apart from their purely personal belongings—considered as a saleable property is not easy to get at all accurately, but it is possible, we think, to obtain a figure which will be at least a useful approximation.

Value of Land.—The great asset of the village people is, of course, the land. The value is difficult to estimate in default of any recent auction sales In their absence we have two means of making an approximate estimation. On the one hand, it has been supposed that the value of the land is represented by twenty-five years' purchase on the Government assessment. Now in this village the average assessment, as we have indicated previously (page 133), is Rs. 1.63. Twenty-five years' purchase on this would be nearly Rs. 41. The best land in the village (classed " 18 annas " in the revenue survey) would be worth Rs. 70 per acre, and that classed as " 16 annas " or, in other words, the best land not possessing abnormal advantages, would be worth Rs. 62 per acre. We are convinced that this figure is considerably too low as is, in fact, clearly indicated by the next method of computation.

A second method of obtaining the value of the land will be to calculate from the amount which money-lenders advance on its security. This is not an absolute test, and it will probably give too high a value, as the land mortgaged will be usually the good land of the village, and usually not that which only grows a poor crop, or no crop at all. The whole of the land mortgaged, however, bears an average burden of Rs. 69 per acre. If we take it that 75 per cent. of the value of land is advanced upon it, this would lead to an estimate of Rs. 92 per acre, an amount more than double that obtained and calculated from the Government assessment.

We believe, however, that this figure is much nearer than that calculated from the assessment, and if the whole cultivable land of the village be taken into account we are inclined to think that an estimate of Rs. 80 as its sale value per acre will not be far from the truth. If anything, this estimate will be too high. If we take this figure, the capital value of the land of the village in its present condition will be Rs. 80,400.

Value of Houses.—If it is difficult to estimate the value of the land, it is even more difficult to obtain what may be called the sale value of the houses in the village. What we are trying to get is, of course, the amount which a purchaser would pay for them, and this would be very little. They represent a good deal of labour, but the actual out-of-pocket expenditure for materials in making them would be small. Most houses are old, and there has been extremely little building in recent years. For a capitalist to build them would cost at least Rs. 500 per house (including the several larger wadas), for 111 households, Rs. 55,500,—but their present sale value cannot exceed Rs. 20,000 and we will take this figure as representing what they are worth at present.

Value of Live Stock.—It is somewhat easier to estimate the value of the 284 head of cattle and buffaloes in the village, and we have already given a figure (Rs. 10,588) on a previous page which may be used in this investigation. The value of the goats can be ignored.

Value of Implements, etc.—As already noted the value of the implements is extraordinarily small, for a complete set of agricultural implements as used in the village is only worth Rs. 39, omitting a cart from consideration.

The actual value of the village stock of implements may be taken (see pages 64 and 66) as follows:—

Larger Implements	Rs.	805
Smaller or hand Implements ..	Rs.	195
Carts	Rs.	1,600
	Rs.	2,600

The whole capital value of the village and its stock, excluding the purely personal possessions of the people, would therefore be—

	Total.		Per cent. of village value.
Land ..	Rs.	80,400	70.8
Houses ..	Rs.	20,000	17.6
Live stock ..	Rs.	10,588	9.3
Implements...	Rs.	2,600	2.3
Total ..	Rs.	1,13,588	

This figure for total value, if it errs at all, is probably, we think, too high.

Even as an approximation such a figure is, however, useful, for it enables us to ascertain the proportion which certain village charges bear to its capital value, and so the relationship which they bear to the conditions prevalent in other countries.

(1) The Government assessment, amounting to Rs. 1,660, is 2.06 per cent. on the value of the land and 1.46 per cent. of the total capital value of the village. The whole

of the compulsory charges on landholders (see page 133) reach 2.8 per cent. of the land value and 2.02 per cent. of the total village valuation.

(2) The average nett return for crops, taking the figure (Rs. 11,823) given on page 114, which, as we have already stated, is probably a little too high, amounts to 14.7 per cent. on the land value and to 10.4 per cent. of the total village value.

(3) The debts of the village (see page 130) amount to Rs. 13,314. Even where the security given is personal, the essential basis on which the debts are incurred is, of course, the property, landed or other, possessed by the people. The debts involve, therefore, an annual charge of 2.28 per cent. against the security on which they are given.

These figures are important and give a vivid idea of the economic position in which the people live.

We have thus described the present condition of the village of Pimpla Soudagar and its people. It illustrates the very great changes which have taken place, and are now taking place, in the position of village communities in the Deccan —changes which have not been very much realised hitherto outside the communities themselves. Formerly a Deccan village was one of the most self-contained units it is possible to conceive. It had its own organisation, village work of almost all kinds was done by recognised village servants who were part of the village arrangements. It governed itself, and had little to do even with the Government when once the revenue was paid. The land was divided into reasonably large holdings, and the produce from the land was sufficient to maintain the whole village population. Some crops were grown—in this case probably wheat chiefly—for outside sale, the money derived being used for things which had necessarily to be obtained outside and to pay the Government assessment. The remainder were for home consumption, and provided there was plenty for this purpose the people did not trouble to intensify the cultivation very much, and so increase the produce. Money rarely passed from hand to hand. In the present case there is no history of subsidiary industries, such as weaving, in the village, but the smallness of the village and the nearness of places like Chinchvad and Poona account for this. But on the whole it was an exceedingly self-sufficing unit and, apart from the incidence of scarcity, it had, like most Deccan villages, little to do with the outside world.

One of the first results of the conditions brought in by the British rule was a gradual increase in the population, and hence under the arrangements usually found under Hindu law, a further sub-division and fragmentation of the land. This led, on the one hand, to a difficulty in maintaining the population as easily as before, and also, we think, probably to the land being, in parts where the fragments were unreasonably small and numerous, worse cultivated than previously. On the other hand, the economic stress undoubtedly led to the introduction of new crops which have given a better return than before.

How far the deterioration in cultivation, due to the fragmentation of the land, prevailed over the improvement brought about by economic stress, we have not the means of ascertaining. The only evidence which makes us think that, on the whole, the class of cultivation has deteriorated is:—

(1) the absence of any new wells. All those existing are old ones and date beyond the present generation.

(2) the absence of newly planted fruit and other trees, which are always an evidence of an active agricultural life. This is the case in spite of the fact that a number of the wells contain ample water for growing and maintaining considerable numbers of fruit trees.

(3) the gradual decrease in the proportion of land which is double-cropped, which amounted (see page 67) to 109 acres in 1885-86, and which only reached an average of 15 acres in the last three years.

These results may perhaps be explained otherwise, but to us they seem to indicate a reduction in the enterprise of the people, though, as we have already said, the introduction of new crops easily marketed and bringing in fairly large money returns would seem to tell in the other direction.

The conditions, however, of increasing population and increasing sub-division of the land were met, in the first instance, by the incurring of debts. How far the present condition of indebtedness is of old standing we have no evidence whatever, nor can we tell how far it has increased in recent years. But to us the debts represent the first effort of the people to meet the changing economic conditions. The difficulties resulting therefrom were, we know, put down to famine,—or rather to climatic changes resulting in greater difficulty of getting good crops. Except in the reduction of late rainfall (October, November, and December) in very recent years, we have failed to find any evidence of such climatic changes. And inasmuch as the climate is nearly always blamed everywhere for agricultural difficulties which cannot be otherwise accounted for, we are inclined to think that the changing conditions of village life (increasing population and increasing fragmentation of land) have probably been at the back of the feeling of unrest with the village conditions which has prevailed, and to the necessity for incurring debts. These debts now form a crushing load amounting to nearly 12 per cent. of the capital value of the village, and the annual charges for them amount to 24.5 per cent. of the total profits from land.

In recent years—the agricultural methods remaining the same and the process of fragmentation of the land being continued—it has become evident to the people that the village can no longer support itself on agriculture, and thus in a continually increasing measure the people have gone outside for work to supplement the earnings from land. The absolute economic necessity for this has been shown and it is significant that we compute that there are only eight out of 103 households* in the village which are self-supporting, at the village standard,

* The total families are 111. It was, however, possible to get sufficient data only from 103.

from land alone. The rest now rely largely on other occupations carried on by some members of the household, and such outside labour has, as a matter of fact, become a much more important source of village income than is the land (see page 129).

In this respect Pimpla Soudagar is peculiar. The proximity of Poona, and particularly of the ammunition factory at Kirkee, has caused the retention of many people and many households in the village who would otherwise have left the village altogether, as residents if not as landowners. The demand for labour is keen elsewhere (Bombay, Poona, etc.), and, under the economic pressure, here met by the Kirkee factory, many of the people in most places leave and go to dwell under urban conditions.* The connection with the village is not at once cut, but it must get feebler, and we have the beginning of a large landless proletariat.

The present village is saved this prospect, at present, it seems, by the fact that work is obtained locally, and the people can work outside and still reside in their ancestral home. But even with this the economic condition is not satisfactory. More than half the families in the village are insolvent according to their own standard of life,—and they must either have less food than they themselves think is absolutely necessary or less clothes than they themselves feel are required, at least for self-respect,—or they must increase their debt.

The position is discouraging, for under these conditions the economic condition must, we feel, be getting worse unless there is a wholesale emigration to towns, which is for many reasons undesirable. If we are asked to place our fingers on the cause (and hence the cure) we can do nothing more than suggest probabilities. Further investigation must disclose how far they represent the real causes.

In the first place, however, it seems to us that the causes of the present position, so far as landowning cultivators are concerned, are partly social, and partly agricultural.

* For illustration see H. H. Mann: *The Mahars of a Deccan Village*; "Social Service Quarterly," Bombay, 1916.

The social cause is the custom of endlessly dividing land, and not merely dividing it, but dividing it in such a way as to lead to the worst possible result, that is to say, to fragmentation into an immense number of extraordinarily small pieces. This destroys enterprise, results in an enormous wastage of labour, leads to a very large loss of land owing to boundaries, makes it impossible to cultivate holdings as intensively as would otherwise be possible, and prevents the possibility of introducing outsiders, with more money, as tenant farmers or as purchasers of a good agricultural property. Some remedy must be found for this condition and some means of preventing it for the future, we feel, if any progress is to be made towards a sounder village life. Whether it will be found in, first, a permissive Act allowing an owner to prevent permanently the sub-division of his self-acquired holding,—leading up to a general measure which will hinder such sub-division on all land for the future; or whether the time is ripe for general arrangements being made for commassation or restriping of land as in many European countries and in Japan, we can hardly tell. A decision in this matter involves an evaluation of how far public opinion is prepared to go, for which the materials do not at present exist.

The second vital cause of the present unsatisfactory state of affairs is the stationary condition of agriculture. This, as we have explained above, results in part from the conditions under which land is cultivated. But, even with this, as will have been noticed in the chapters dealing with the village crops, there is little evidence of progressive agriculture. Without such progressive agriculture we feel the population is too great for the land. With progressive methods we are not at all sure that even a dry village like Pimpla Soudagar could not support a larger population than it at present has. There seems, as one goes about the village, to be great room for improvement without a serious increase of out-of-pocket expenditure, and only requiring more labour better applied. This intensification of agriculture has hardly commenced.

The stimulus for it must come from outside, but if properly applied we are certain that improvements would be welcome and carried out. At present, however, the Agricultural Department is small, its investigations on the best methods of dealing with dry land, and especially with dry shallow land on the Deccan, are only in a very early stage. It will have to be increased both as to its investigating staff and as to its district staff to an enormous extent before the thousands of similar villages similar to Pimpla Soudagar can come under the influence of progressive methods.

These causes seem the essential factors in producing the present unsatisfactory condition of the village. There are others which are subsidiary, but equally important. The lack of capital, except the land, and the high rate at which capital can be obtained; the relative uncertainty of dry cultivation even in this part of the Deccan and hence the apparent pity that such large quantities of water should pass unutilised by the village site; the poor agricultural stock which cause cultivation and agriculture generally to be conducted in an uneconomic manner; and the all but total lack of village organisation to produce the greatest return from the land or to prevent economic waste,—all these are vital, but seem to be in large measure included in the major social and agricultural causes already considered.

The present is not a time to go a step further and suggest how these causes of the unsatisfactory character of the village as an economic unit should be combated. We have not yet determined how far the village is typical of the dry villages of the western Deccan. We believe it is typical, and as such we have described it, but further investigation is necessary before large and extensive schemes of dealing with the situation can be devised and brought into effect. Further, we have not determined to our own satisfaction the relative importance to be attached to the various factors in the economic situation—and this again requires very much more extended enquiry of a similar sort in other Deccan villages.

But the study we have made and the results to which we have come are such as to cause profound suspicion that the condition, at least of our dry agricultural villages, is much less satisfactory than has been usually considered. The next need is for further inquiry. If our results and conclusions are confirmed it would appear that the situation is one towards the alteration of which a very large part of the attention of the public and the action of the authorities should be devoted.

APPENDIX A.

Analyses of River Water at Pimpla Soudagar.

(See page 21.)

River Water : before the *nala* joins the river.

	Nov. 1913	Jan. 1914	March 1914	May 1914	Aug. 1914	Oct. 1914
		Parts per 100,000				
Total soluble salts	35.0	25.0	27.0	32.0	34.0	40.0
Containing—						
Calcium carbonate	14.0	10.0	12.0	6.0	6.0	4.0
Magnesium carbonate ..	6.1	9.5	2.5	8.6	12.1	9.1
Magnesium sulphate.. ..	5.6	1.5	3.5	2.6	..	..
Magnesium chloride	.6	..	4.8	..	..	..
Sodium carbonate	.7	..	6.3	6.3	..	..
Sodium bicarbonate	..	..	..	..	3.0	12.7
Sodium sulphate	..	..	..	1.7	4.8	3.6
Sodium chloride	4.0	3.5	..	7.1	4.7	4.7

River Water : after the *nala* joins the river.

	Nov. 1913	Jan. 1914	March 1914	Aug. 1914	Oct. 1914
	Parts per 100,000				
Total soluble salts	32.0	26.0	31.0	16.0	24.0
Containing—					
Calcium carbonate	14.0	10.0	9.0	6.0	2.0
Magnesium carbonate	6.9	8.7	4.5	2.5	4.5
Magnesium sulphate	3.1	1.5	..	..	..
Magnesium chloride	0.8	0.9	..	3.9	..
Sodium carbonate	1.4	..	6.3	..	2.1
Sodium bicarbonate	..	..	2.1	..	8.9
Sodium sulphate	..	..	0.6	..	..
Sodium chloride	1.3	2.4	4.7	..	4.7

APPENDIX B.

Analyses of Well Water at Pimpla Soudagar.

(See pages 22 to 31.)

Well No. 1 (Survey No. 176.)

	Nov. 1913	Jan. 1914	March 1914	May 1914	Aug. 1914	Oct. 1914
		Parts per 100,000				
Total soluble salts	40.0	38.0	34.0	32.0	32.0	40.0
Containing—						
Calcium carbonate	10.0	10.0	14.0	10.0	6.0	10.0
Magnesium carbonate ..	4.5	7.6	5.6	7.6	7.6	9.1
Magnesium sulphate ..	..	..	1.5	..	..	..
Magnesium chloride ..	..	..	1.1	..	..	..
Sodium carbonate	..	..	4.2	..	..	..
Sodium bicarbonate ..	13.1	10.0	..	4.2	7.5	7.7
Sodium sulphate	4.8	3.0	..	2.4	.6	2.4
Sodium chloride	3.5	3.5	1.0	4.7	7.1	5.9

Well No. 2 (Survey No. 180.)

	Nov. 1913	Jan. 1914	March 1914	May 1914	Aug. 1914	Oct. 1914
		Parts per 100,000				
Total soluble salts	53.0	46.0	40.0	32.0	44.0	44.0
Containing—						
Calcium carbonate	16.0	4.0	4.0	6.0	12.0	14.0
Magnesium carbonate ..	10.5	5.8	8.8	9.1	10.6	12.5
Magnesium sulphate	..	..	..	..	..	..
Magnesium chloride	..	..	..	..	..	..
Sodium carbonate	..	3.1	4.2	3.1	..	..
Sodium bicarbonate ..	6.8	19.4	8.4	2.8	6.4	7.4
Sodium sulphate	7.3	3.0	4.2	2.4	2.4	2.4
Sodium chloride	7.1	4.9	5.9	4.7	9.5	7.1

Well No. 3 (Survey No. 150).

	Nov. 1913	Jan. 1914	March 1914	May 1914	Aug. 1914	Oct. 1914
		Parts per 100,000				
Total soluble salts	49.0	47.0	42.0	44.0	40.0	44.0
Containing—						
Calcium carbonate	16.0	13.0	12.0	6.0	10.0	6.0
Magnesium carbonate ..	11.4	3.0	4.5	9.1	9.1	3.0
Magnesium sulphate	..	..	..	..	..	..
Magnesium chloride	..	..	..	..	..	..
Sodium carbonate	..	..	4.2	..	4.2	..
Sodium bicarbonate	7.6	21.2	12.2	21.1	9.3	22.4
Sodium sulphate	5.4	0.6	0.6	1.2	2.4	3.6
Sodium chloride	5.9	4.7	4.7	7.1	4.7	7.1

Well No. 4 (Survey No. 159).

	Nov. 1913	Jan. 1914	March 1914	May 1914	Aug. 1914	Oct. 1914
		Parts per 100,000				
Total soluble salts	36.0	35.0	51.0	32.0	40.0	44.0
Containing—						
Calcium carbonate	9.0	10.0	16.0	8.0	8.0	10.0
Magnesium carbonate.. ..	3.8	6.8	8.3	7.6	9.1	6.0
Magnesium sulphate	..	..	..	2.0	..	..
Magnesium chloride	..	..	..	..	..	..
Sodium carbonate	..	..	5.3	2.1	1.0	..
Sodium bicarbonate	13.0	9.9	10.7	..	9.3	14.1
Sodium sulphate	3.6	.6	1.8	..	2.4	2.4
Sodium chloride	3.5	4.7	4.7	7.1	4.7	4.7

Well No. 5 (Survey No. 136).

	Nov. 1913	Jan. 1914	March 1914	May 1914	Aug. 1914	Oct. 1914
		Parts per 100,000				
Total soluble salts	51.0	51.0	53.0	60.0	52.0	48.0
Containing—						
Calcium carbonate	6.0	7.0	2.0	4.0	6.0	12.0
Magnesium carbonate ..	7.6	8.3	6.8	13.7	15.2	3.2
Magnesium sulphate	..	..	..	..	..	....
Magnesium chloride	..	..	..	..	..	..
Sodium carbonate	..	4.2	16.9	..	4.2	4.2
Sodium bicarbonate	23.1	21.1	16.8	24.0	16.8	15.2
Sodium sulphate	3.0	0.6	2.4	2.4	..	..
Sodium chloride	5.9	5.9	5.9	8.3	5.9	7.1

Well No. 6 (Survey No. 124).

	Nov. 1913	Jan. 1914	March 1914	May 1914	Aug. 1914	Oct. 1914
		Parts per 100,000				
Total soluble salts	31.0	35.0	39.0	28.0	28.0	36.0
Containing—						
Calcium carbonate	19.0	11.0	19.0	2.0	6.0	14.0
Magnesium carbonate ..	7.6	9.9	5.2	9.1	7.6	9.1
Magnesium sulphate	1.0	..	4.6	..	..	..
Magnesium chloride	..	..	1.0	..	..	..
Sodium carbonate	..	..	2.1	..	6.3	14.0
Sodium bicarbonate	..	5.6	..	6.0	..	4.3
Sodium sulphate	..	.6	..	1.2	..	..
Sodium chloride	3.5	4.7	2.3	4.7	3.5	4.7

Well No. 7 (Survey No. 71.)

	Nov. 1913	Jan. 1914	March 1914	May 1914	Aug. 1914	Oct. 1914
			Parts per 100,000			
Total soluble salts	41.0	29.0	28.0	36.0	28.0	28.0
Containing—						
Calcium carbonate	11.0	7.0	1.0	8.0	12.0	6.0
Magnesium carbonate	9.7	3.0	4.5	7.6	10.6	6.0
Magnesium sulphate	..	..	..	..	..	..
Magnesium chloride	..	..	..	..	..	..
Sodium carbonate	..	..	4.2	..	..	..
Sodium bicarbonate	0.6	8.6	8.0	10.9	..	7.4
Sodium sulphate	9.7	0.6	0.6	..	..	1.2
Sodium chloride	7.1	5.9	7.1	7.1	4.7	4.7

Well No. 8 (Survey No. 27).

	Nov. 1913	Jan. 1914	March 1914	May 1914	Aug. 1914	Oct. 1914
			Parts per 100,000			
Total soluble salts	19.0	12.0	15.0	28.0	12.0	16.0
Containing—						
Calcium carbonate	4.0	3.0	7.0	14.0	2.0	4.0
Magnesium carbonate	3.1	1.2	1.7	8.4	2.8	3.8
Magnesium sulphate	2.5	..	0.5	..	..	2.0
Magnesium chloride	1.3	..	..	.7	..	..
Sodium carbonate	2.9	..	3.7	..	..	..
Sodium bicarbonate	..	4.4	..	..	0.7	..
Sodium sulphate	..	0.6	..	..	..	..
Sodium chloride	1.9	2.3	1.9	2.7	3.5	4.7

Well No. 9 (Survey No. 31).

	Nov. 1913	Jan. 1914	March 1914	May 1914	Aug. 1914	Oct. 1914
	Parts per 100,000					
Total soluble salts	43.0	28.0	24.0	28.0	40.0	36.0
Containing—						
Calcium carbonate	12.0	10.0	12.0	12.0	10.0	12.0
Magnesium carbonate ..	6.9	9.1	0.8	6.7	10.6	3.0
Magnesium sulphate	..	..	1.5	1.5	..	..
Magnesium chloride	..	..	2.9	2.9	..	..
Magnesia in other forms ..	..	..	2.0	..	..	..
Sodium carbonate	..	..	3.1	4.2	..	..
Sodium bicarbonate	2.5	4.3	..	..	1.1	12.0
Sodium sulphate	8.5	1.8	..	..	6.1	3.6
Sodium chloride	5.9	3.5	..	..	7.1	3.5

Well No. 10 (Survey No. 40).

	Nov. 1913	Jan. 1914	March 1914	May 1914	Aug. 1914	Oct. 1914
	Parts per 100,000					
Total soluble salts	38.0	34.0	26.0	44.0	34.0	32.0
Containing—						
Calcium carbonate	10.0	6.0	12.0	10.0	8.0	12.0
Magnesium carbonate ..	5.3	7.6	5.9	3.0	4.5	10.6
Magnesium sulphate	..	..	1.0	..	..	..
Magnesium chloride	..	..	1.1	..	..	..
Sodium carbonate	..	..	2.1	..	..	..
Sodium bicarbonate	9.0	10.9	..	10.2	8.8	2.8
Sodium sulphate	4.8	1.2	..	2.4	3.6	..
Sodium chloride	4.7	4.7	3.4	9.5	4.7	5.9

Well No. 11 (Survey No. 50).

	Nov. 1913	Jan. 1914	March 1914	May 1914	Aug. 1914	Oct. 1914
		Parts per 100,000				
Total soluble salts	39.0	32.0	35.0	32.0	46.0	36.0
Containing—						
Calcium carbonate	13.0	15.0	12.0	10.0	10.0	12.0
Magnesium carbonate ..	9.7	5.9	1.7	7.6	3.0	12.3
Magnesium sulphate	..	1.0	6.1	..	..	..
Magnesium chloride	..	1.1	3.7	..	..	..
Sodium carbonate	..	2.1	7.4	..	..	..
Sodium bicarbonate	3.7	..	..	7.5	13.7	2.8
Sodium sulphate	3.6	..	..	..	7.3	..
Sodium chloride	4.7	3.3	0.5	4.7	7.1	5.9

APPENDIX C.

RECORD AND DECISION OF THE *Inam* COMMISSION RELATING TO THE *Inam* OF PIMPLA SOUDAGAR GRANTED TO RANGO PANDIT KHOLE.

(See page 38).

Report No. 107. *Dated at Poona, the* 30*th April* 1856.

Collectorate Poona, Talook Huweillee,

Village—Pimplay Sowdagur.

Claimant.—Ruckmajee oorf Rowjee bin Amrut Row bin Rungo Punt Kholey.

Claim.—The entire village, except ancient Hucks and Inams, free of assessment until the death of the last surviving son of Rungo Punt ; after which one half the village as an hereditary Inam.

Entered in the Chittas, etc., of the present Government for 1850-1 as the " sherakuttee " (partially alienated) village of Rungo Bappoojee Kholey.

1. *Particulars and date of Grant as stated by the claimant* :—Granted in Inam in 1819 by the Honourable Mr. Elphinstone, when Commissioner in the Deccan, to claimant's grandfather Rungo Bappoojee as a reward for his useful services.

2. *Occupant at the introduction of the present Government, as stated by the claimant* :—The village has been acquired since 1817-1818.

3. *Number of years and descents through which it would appear from claimant's statement the Inam had been continued previous to the introduction of the present Government* :——years —descents.

4. *Particulars of the history of the alleged Inam since the introduction of the present Government, as stated by the claimant* :—The village has continued to be enjoyed in *Inam*.

5. *Description of the evidence produced by the claimant in support of his title* :—Seven documents purporting to be :

I. A sunnud, dated the 9th June 1819, from Captain Henry Dundas Robertson, Collector of Poona, to the address of Rungo Bappooji Kholey Banekar, as follows :—" As a reward for the services you have performed under Captain Briggs, Collector of Khandesh, the entire village of Pimplay Sowdagur, except its ancient Hucks and Inams in the Haweillee Turuff of the Poona Prant, is hereby granted to you in Inam, to be enjoyed by you and by your sons, that is to say, for two generations."

II. A similar document addressed to the District Officers (Deshmookh and Deshpandey) of Turuff Haweillee, Prant Poona.

III. A similar document addressed to the village officers (Mokuddums) of Pimplay Sowdagur.

IV. A sunnud, dated the 22nd July 1819, from the Honourable Mount Stewart Elphinstone to the comavisdars (Revenue managers), District Officers (Deshmook and Deshpandey), and village officers (Mokuddums) of Pimplay Sowdagar, Turuff Huweillee of Soobha Poona, to the following effect :—" Rungo Bappooji Kholey Banekar has solicited, wherefore, taking into consideration the useful services rendered by him in Khandesh, the entire village of Pimplay Sowdagur, except its Hucks and Inams and the customs (Zukat) in the Huweillee Turuff of Prant Poona, is hereby granted to him in Inam by the Government. The village is therefore to be made over to him accordingly and continued to him and to his sons, or for two generations."

V. A letter, dated 26th July 1819, from Captain John Briggs, (Political Agent) of Khandesh, to Rungo Punt Kholey, forwarding to him the sunnud last recited. . . . .

VI. A *Takeed* (letter of injunction), dated 4th August 1819, from the Mamlatdar of Pargana Haweillee of Poona, directing the village officers of Pimplay to make over that village to the enjoyment of Rungo Bappooji according to the sunad, which had been issued on the subject, the village was to be continued for two generations.

VII. The subjoined geneological table :—

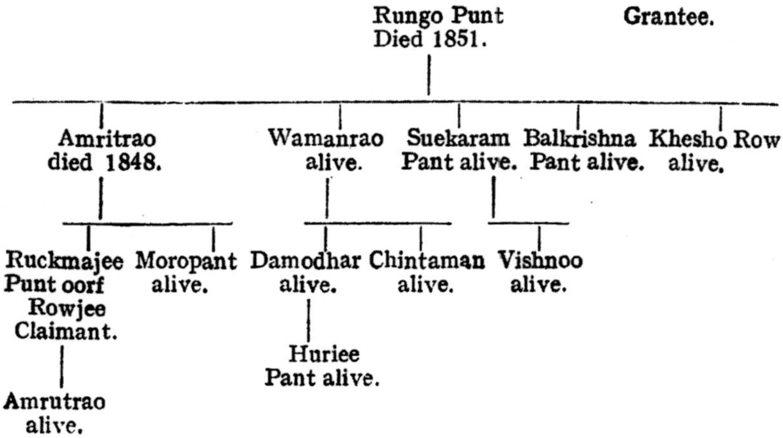

6. The history of the claim under enquiry appears to be as follows :—

7. On the 7th December 1818 Captain Briggs, the Political Agent in Khandesh, wrote a letter to the Honourable M. Elphinstone, Commissioner in the Deccan, explaining the arrangements and settlements he had made in the District. Captain Briggs observed :—

" . . I consider it a duty I owe to the individuals who have afforded me such zealous assistance to bring their merits particularly to your notice with a hope that you will be disposed to recommend to Government some permanent reward for their services.". . . . .

" Rungo Pundit, a respectable Brahmin of Poona with whom I had some acquaintance while there : he was detached at the same time with 300 auxiliary horse and an advance of Rs. 5,000 to occupy the Gungterry ; his activity and personal acquaintance with many of the killadars of the forts, as well as a considerable share of address, enabled him to occupy almost without resistance all the plain. . . . . I beg to propose that they should each have grants of such villages in the vicinity of their houses as they themselves might select, to descend in one generation to their children and afterwards to be held by their posterity in perpetuity at an assessment equal to half the present rate............ I beg leave to suggest the following value of the village for Rungo Pundit, a village whose *tunkhah* shall not exceed 2,000 rupees."

8. On the 13th December 1818 the above letter from Captain Briggs was submitted by the Honourable Mr. Elphinstone for the orders of the Government of India with a recommendation........

9. The subjoined reply by the Government of India, January 1819:—"The Governor-General in Council has directed me to acknowledge the receipt of your despatch of the 13th ultimo and to convey to you His Excellency's sanction for the grant recommended by Captain Briggs to be made to........ Rungo Pundit."

10. The latest State records of the Peshwa's Government showing the value of the village of Pimplay Sowdagur, before it was made over to the present claimant's grandfather, are accounts for six years commencing with 1806-07 and ending with 1811-12. The average amount of revenue annually derived from the village during those years is shown by the following accounts to have been as follows :—

Gross revenue	Rs.	1,024	11	4
Expenses	Rs.	311	4	11
Balance of nett revenue	Rs.	713	6	5

11. The subjoined abstract of the distribution of the revenue of the village for the year 1818-19:—

Kumal or highest recorded assessment of the village	Rs.	1,102	0	0
Amount of gross revenue realised from the village for 1818-19 A.D.	Rs.	1,103	0	0
Deduct expenses	Rs.	193	0	0
Balance of nett revenue	Rs.	910	0	0
One-half of which is	Rs.	455	0	0

12. The Assistant Inam Commissioner's decision, therefore, as follows :—The village of Pimplay Sowdagur, after deducting its ancient Hucks and Inams, is to be continued free from assessment for so long as any one of the four persons may be alive. From the date of the death of the last survivor the village is to be continued for so long as there may be in existence any male descendant in male lineage of the Grantee, Rungo Pant, subject to an annual payment to Government of Rupees four hundred and fifty-five (455), this being one-half the amount at which the village was assessed in 1818-19 A.D. when the grant was made.—Act XI of 1852, Schedule B, Rule 1.

APPENDIX D.

LIST OF HERBACEOUS PLANTS IN VILLAGE OF PIMPLA SOUDAGAR.

Botanical Name.	Natural Order.	Marathi Name.	Situation.	Remarks.
I. *Very Common Plants*—				
(1) *Sida spinosa*	Malvaceæ	..	In fields and on borders of fields.	A small branched shrub with small yellow flowers.
(2) *Triumfetta rotundifolia*	Tiliaceæ	*Landaga*	On the borders of fields.	A small shrubby plant with small round spiny fruits sticking to the clothes.
(3) *Heylandia latebrosa*	Leguminoseæ	*Godhadi*	....	A prostrate, much branched herb, liked by cattle.
(4) *Cassia Tora*	do.	*Takla*	In waste places.	....
(5) *Indigofera glandulosa*	do.	*Barbada*	In fields and on the borders.	Small erect plants with black dots on the under side of leaves. Cattle are fond of the plant.
(6) *Psoralia corylifolia*	do.	*Bavachi*	In waste places.	The plant is eaten by cattle.
(7) *Vernonia cinerea*	Compositæ	..	On borders of fields.	Seeds easily scattered by wind.
(8) *Launaea nudicaulis*	do.	*Pathari*	In the fields.	The seeds are very easily scattered about by wind.
(9) *Convolvulus arvensis*	Convolvulaceæ	*Chandvel*	In fields	....

Botanical Name.	Natural Order.	Marathi Name.	Situation.	Remarks.
(10) *Solanum melongena*	Solanaceæ	*Ranwanga*	On borders of fields.	Probably run wild.
(11) *Justicia diffusa*	Acanthaceæ	*Kalmashi*	In the fields.	....
(12) *Euphorbia hypori-cifolia var. parviflora*	Euphorbiaceæ	..	In fields.	....
(13) *Euphorbia thymifolia*	do.	*Dhakti dudhi*	In fields.	....
(14) *Cynodon dactylon*	Gramineæ	*Hariali*	Wherever moisture is available.	Eaten by cattle. A troublesome weed.
(15) *Panicum Isachne*	do.	*Shimpi*	In fields.	Eaten by cattle. A troublesome weed.
(16) *Andropogon annulatus*	do.	*Marvel*	On borders of fields	Eaten by cattle.
(17) *Andropogon caricosus var mollicornis*	do.	do.	do.	do.
(18) *Ischaemum pilosum*	do.	*Kunda*	In fields.	Eaten by cattle. A troublesome weed.
(19) *Ischaemunm sulcatum*	do.	..	On borders of fields.	Eaten by cattle.
(20) *Eragrostis interrupta*	do.	..	In moist places.	....
(21) *Dinebra arabica*	do.	..	In fields.	Eaten by cattle.
(22) *Pennisetum sp.*	do.	*Mohl*	Along the streams.	....
II. Common Plants—				
(1) *Corchorus trilocularis*	Tiliaceæ	*Kadu chinch*	On the borders of fields.	....

Botanical Name.	Natural Order.	Marathi Name.	Situation.	Remarks.
(2) *Indigofera linifolia*	Leguminseæ	*Pandar phalli*	On the borders of fields.	....
(3) *Phaseolus trilobus*	do.	*Mukni : jangli Math*	do.	....
(4) *Ammannia banifora*	Lythraceæ	*Bhar jambhul*	In moist places.	....
(5) *Eclipta erecta*	Compositæ	*Maka*	....	....
(6) *Echinops echinatus*	do.	*Utkatari*	On borders of fields.	Seeds scattered by wind.
(7) *Tridax procumbens*	do.	....	do.	do.
(8) *Exacusa pedunculatum*	Gentianaceæ	....	In moist places,	A small herb with dark blue flowers.
(9) *Ipomaea reniformis*	Convolvulaceæ	*Underkani*	do.	....
(10) *Solanum nigrum*	Solanaceæ	*Kanguni*	On borders of fields.	....
(11) *Nicandra physaloides*	do.	*Ranpopti*	do.	....
(12) *Physalis minima*	do.	do.	do.	....
(13) *Achyranthes aspera*	Amarantaceæ	*Aghada*	On borders of fields.	A troublesome weed.
(14) *Cyperus rotundus*	Cyperaceæ	*Nagarmotha*	In moist places,	Eaten by buffaloes. A troublesome weed.
(15) *Apluda varia*	Gramineæ	..	In bushes.	Eaten by cattle.
(16) *Paspalum Sanguinale vaciliare*	do.	*Rewga*	....	do.
(17) *Andropogon pumillus*	do.	*Gondwal*	In fallow fields.	do.

Botanical Name.	Natural Order.	Marathi Name.	Situation.	Remarks.
III. Fairly Common Plants—				
(1) *Argemone mexicana*	Papaveraceæ	*Piwla dhotra*	In waste places.	A herb with prickly leaves and large yellow flowers.
(2) *Tribulus terrestris*	Zygophyllaceæ	*Sarata*	....	Fruits used medicinally.
(3) *Alysicarpus rugosus*	Leguminosæ	*Shewra*	....	A small plant with pink flowers and small jointed wrinkled pods.
(4) *Blainvillea latifolia*	Compositæ	..	....	....
(5) *Goniocaulon glabrum*	do.	*Kadkusumba*	On borders of fields.	....
(6) *Flaveria contrayerba*	do.	..	In fields.	Leaves 3 nerved; heads with small yellow flowers.
(7) *Hemigraphis dura*	Acanthaceæ	*Gantilbu*	On borders of fields.	A bristly straggling plant with blue flowers.
(8) *Ocimum canum*	Labiatæ	*Rantulsi*	In waste places.	....
(9) *Cyanotis axillaris*	Commelinaceæ	..	In fields.	Eaten by cattle.
(10) *Commelina* sp.	do.	..	do.	....
(11) *Arthraxon lanceolatus*	Gramineæ	..	On hard soil.	Eaten by cattle.
(12) *Andropogon monticolus*	do.	..	On hard soil.	do.
(13) *Eragrostis pilosa*	do.	..	In moist places.	Relished by buffaloes.
IV. Plants found frequently—				
(1) *Cocculus villosus*	Menispermaceæ	*Vasanwel*	In the middle of fields.	A straggling scandent plant with softly hairy leaves.

Botanical Name.	Natural Order.	Marathi Name.	Situation.	Remarks.
(2) *Polygala chinensis*	Polygalaceæ	*Phutani*	In the middle of fields.	A small herb with small yellow flowers.
(3) *Portulaca oleracea*	Portulaceæ	*Ghol*	....	A small herb with small succulent leaves.
(4) *Indigofera trita*	Leguminoscæ	..	On borders of fields.	....
(5) *Desmodium diffusum*	do.	*Chikta*	....	Greedily eaten by cattle.
(6) *Rhynchosia minima*	do.	..	....	
(7) *Indigofera cordifolia*	do.	*Godhadi*	....	Buffaloes are fond of this plant.
(8) *Pulicaria wightiana*	Compositæ	..	....	Heads large, yellow flowered.
(9) *Vicea auriculata*	do.	*Sonkadi*	....	....
(10) *Sonchus arvensis*	do.	..	In the fields.	The seeds are very easily scattered by wind.
(11) *Lactuca remotiflora*	do.	*Pathari*	do.	do.
(12) *Blumea eriantha*	do.	*Nimurdi*	On borders of fields.	....
(13) *Sutera glandulosa*	Scrophulariaceæ	*Bhul*	In waste places.	A small vicoid herb with a cool sensation on touching it. Flowers small white.
(14) *Celosia argentea*	Amarantaceæ	*Kurdu*	On borders of fields.	An erect plant with conspicuous showy pink spikes.
(15) *Digera arvensis*	do.	..	In fields.	....
(16) *Euphorbia Rothiana*	Euphorbiaceæ	*Dudhi*	do.	....

Botanical Name.	Natural Order.	Marathi Name.	Situation.	Remarks.
(17) *Euphorbia dracunculoides*	Euphorbiaceæ	*Dudhi*	In fields.	....
(18) *Iseilema laxum*	Gramineæ	..	....	Eaten by cattle.
V. *Plants not Common*—				
(1) *Bergia ammannioides*	Elalineæ	..	In moist places.	....
(2) *Hibiscus panduraeformis*	Malvaceæ	..	....	....
(3) *Hibiscus ficulneus*	do.	..	....	Yields excellent fibre.
(4) *Corchorus olitorius*	Tiliaceæ	*Banpat*	....	Yields good fibre.
(5) *Biophytum sensitivum*	Geraniaceæ	..	....	....
(6) *Zizyphus xylopyra*	Rhamnaceæ	..	On borders of fields.	A small thorny shurb.
(7) *Prosopis spicigera*	Leguminoseæ	*Sanndad*	On borders of fields.	....
(8) *Alysicarpus tetragonolobus*	do.	..	....	A small plant with pink flowers and small jointed wrinkled pods.
(9) *Crotalaria orixensis*	do.	*Andbail*	....	....
(10) *Sesbania aculeata*	do.	*Ran Shevri*	In moist places.	....
(11) *Crotalaria linifolia*	do.	..	....	Eaten by cattle.
(12) *Crotalaria retusa*	do.	*Dingala*	....	....
(13) *Indigofera trifoliata*	do.	..	....	Somewhat like 5 in I, but with an angular pod.

Botanical Name.	Natural Order.	Marathi Name.	Situation.	Remarks.
(14) *Mimosa hamata*	Leguminosæ	*Arati*	On borders of fields.	A small shrub with pink heads of flowers and prickly pods.
(15) *Crotalaria vestita*	do.	..	....	....
(16) *Cucumis trigonus*	Cucurbitaceæ	*Karit*	In fields.	....
(17) *Oldenlandia aspera*	Rubiaceæ	..	do.	....
(18) *Spermacoce stricta*	do.	..	do.	....
(19) *Tricholepis radicans*	Compositæ	*Dahan*	On borders of fields.	Seeds easily scattered by wind.
(20) *Caesulia axillaris*	do.	*Maka*	....	....
(21) *Xanthium strumarium*	do.	*Sankeshwar*	do.	A plant with large toothed leaves and spiny fruits of the size of the pod of gram.
(22) *Marsdenia lanceolata*	Asclepiadaceæ	..	In fields.	....
(23) *Marsdenia volubilis*	do.	*Hiran*	On the side of fields.	Cattle are said to eat the leaves.
(24) *Erythrea Roxburghii*	Gentianaceæ	*Luntak*	....	....
(25) *Trichodesma zeylanicum*	Boragineæ	..	....	A scabrid erect plant with hanging ball-shaped flowers.
(26) *Ipomaea eriocarpa*	Convolvulaceæ	..	In fields.	Smothers jowar plant by twining round it.

Botanical Name.	Natural Order	Marathi Name.	Situation.	Remarks.
(27) *Solanum xanthocarpum*	Solanaceæ	*Bhuiringni : kateringni*	In fields.	The root is used medicinally.
(28) *Datura alba*	do.	*Dhotra*	In waste places.	....
(29) *Stenodia viscosa*	Scrophulariaceæ	..	In moist places.	....
(30) *Rungia elegans*	Acanthaceæ	..	On borders of fields.	....
(31) *Leucas aspera*	Labiatæ	..	do.	....
(32) *Lavandula burmanii*	do.	*Ghodeghui*	do.	....
(33) *Leucas martinicensis*	do.	..	do.	....
(34) *Phyllanthus waderaspatensis*	Euphorbiaceæ	..	In fields.	....
(35) *Acalypha malabarica*	do.	..	do.	....
(36) *Euphorbia geniculata*	do.	..	In waste places.	....
(37) *Chrozophora plicata*	do.	*Suryavarti*	In moist places.	....
(38) *Asparagus racemous*	Liliaceæ	*Shatavari*	On borders of fields.	....
(39) *Chlorophytum sp.*	do.	*Kulai*	....	....
(40) *Eragrostis minor*	Gramineæ	..	....	....
(41) *Arthraxon merboldii*	do.	..	....	....
(42) *Anthisteria ciliata*	do.	..	....	Eaten by cattle.
(43) *Ophiurus corymbosus*	do.	..	....	Eaten by cattle when young.
(44) *Sporobolus diander*	do.	..	....	Eaten by cattle.
(45) *Andropogon triticeus.*	do.	..	On borders of fields.	....

Botanical Name.	Natural Order.	Marathi Name.	Situation.	Remarks.
***VI.** Plants escaped from cultivation—*				
(1) *Brassica juncea*	Cruciferæ	*Raimohori*	....	An escape from cultivation.
(2) *Hibiscus cannabinus*	Malvaceæ	*Ambadi*	....	do.
(3) *Linum usitatissimum*	Linaceæ	*Alshi*	....	do.
(4) *Cajanus indicus*	Leguminoseæ	*Tur*	....	do.
(5) *Pisum sativum*	do.	*Watana*	....	do.
(6) *Phaseolus mungo*	do.	*Udid*	....	do.
(7) *Pencedanum gramolus*	Umbelliferæ	*Balantshep*	....	do.
(8) *Foeniculum vulgare*	do.	*Badishep*	....	do.
(9) *Daucus carota*	do.	*Gajar*	....	do.
(10) *Sesamum indicum*	Pedalineæ	*Til*	....	do.

INDEX.

C—(Contd.)

D

E

F

G

H

I

J

K

K—(Contd.)

L

M

P—(Contd.)

R

S

S—(Contd.)

T

T—(Contd.)

U

V

W

Z